OLD REDDITCH
A Walk Back in Time

OLD REDDITCH

A Walk Back in Time

By

Lily Norris

BREWIN BOOKS

First published
by Brewin Books, Studley, Warwickshire, B80 7LG
in June 1993

© Lily Norris

ISBN 1 85858 022 6

British Library Cataloguing in Publication Data.
A Catalogue record for this book is available from the British Library

Typeset by Avon Dataset, Bidford on Avon, Warwickshire, B50 4JH
and made and printed by Supaprint (Redditch) Limited.

Contents

A Sunday School Teacher

I Dedicate the Book "Old Redditch"

To my Dear friend and chum John Edmund Tucker for assistance and patience while writing the text.

Acknowledgements: Old Moore's Almanack,
Marjorie Rust
Redditch Indicator
Mr Jack Lewis

And other kind people of Redditch who have submitted material to be used in this book for the present time and for posterity.

Withybed Green

My dad told us we were going to Feather Bed Lane every time we enquired of our next move. My mother vowed this was to be our last upheaval. This was a strange oath for my mother, being the youngest and last born of the famous and much-respected James William Chipperfield she was always willing to obey the inborn love of travelling. Exploring new places, meeting friendly, interesting people and challenging different situations that each day would bring was an urge that usually could not be denied.

Nevertheless, with such a large family travelling became much more difficult. That is how we eventually settled towards the end of the Great War in this tiny hamlet a long, stony mile south of Alvechurch, called Withybed Green. After the dust, noise and crowds of people in Birmingham where we previously lived it seemed like Paradise to us children. There was fishing from the nearby canal, endless trees to climb and woods and spinneys full of treasures we had never before touched. The nature spot near the brook on the left-hand side up the Birches was a gem. Early spring brought a fine display of delicate, green spurs of promised bluebells, aconites and fronds of sweet-smelling ferns.

The local brickyard provided employment for most of the local people, including several women although this heavy brick and tile-making in the hot kilns was definitely not women's work, but it seemed the only other employment available at that time was in Redditch about seven miles away.

My father, Ernest Cater, born in Bridgenorth, came from a long line of engineers, his father inventing a revolutionary loom for the carpet factory in Kidderminster. There remained until recently a street called Cater Street in recognition of his work. Taught by their father the intricate workings of the traction engines, my brothers, James, Ernest and John Llewellyn were all able to drive the monsters at an early age. One day the three young lads were out delivering a load of bricks to a firm in Redditch when they were stopped by the law. A policeman fetched my father from the yard and queried the boys' ages and insisted that they were unable to control the engine, whereupon my father asked the policeman to move it, but the startled officer admitted that he was helpless with machinery and that no way could he move the blessed thing to which my father said "You can't drive it but they can. Right lads carry on and take this load to Bryants Yard as planned." James, the eldest was only sixteen.

No public transport was available, so the locals who worked in the needle factories in Redditch had no option but to walk a good mile along the tow-path to get the train or about the same distance to take a Midland Red bus by walking down the winding village lane. We children were elated every Monday morning for a Lavender Laundry van called at The Crown public house to collect the weekly washing so instead of having to negotiate that long stony lane we were given a lift. There was plenty of whoops and shouts "The Laundry van is here". He dropped us off at the church gates and from there we dawdled past the elm trees full of calling crows and down the 'black path'. Unfortunately these elm trees have been removed and gone also are the familiar sounds of the crows.

Nearing the end of the 'black path' if we could hear Miss James playing the morning hymns it was a signal that we were late and, as a group, we raced like hell.

Mr Tom Kirby, our headmaster, wore a wig as a result of war injuries, and sometimes, when tempers frayed, it would slide over his one eye. He was very strict but his mode of teaching stayed forever in my mind. No child was released from his lessons until through constant repetition every word was imprinted on our books and on our memory.

Tom Kirby was always fair-minded but his crabbed expression portrayed the suffering he had seen in the battle of the Western Front. Although this did not excuse his nasty behaviour towards the older girls for which he was dismissed long after we went to Webheath to live. Thank God we younger pupils escaped. Miss James and Mrs Edmunds eventually investigated the complaints from Hilda Gwyn, Nellie South Hetty Groves and several other girls in the top class. This is one of the shades of grey we find in an otherwise delightful era.

Cyril Hopkins, a good teacher, and wonderful organiser. All the class were treated to a glorious day's enjoyment. It began with a gloomy mist that rose from the canal banks like foamy cotton-wool. My mother said 'It's going to be a scorcher.' First we travelled to the Malvern hills where we released our stored energy, then onto the town of Worcester, but my most tender memory is sitting in the cheerful sunshine of the friendly town of Tewkesbury. To this day there still remains the unforgettable taste of delicate chicken sandwiches served at the picnic on that idyllic outing. We thanked Mr Hopkins and presented him with a modest bunch of flowers for his wife who, unfortunately, always seemed poorly. But I'm sure his reward was seeing the coach load of happy, laughing very tired children at the end of a perfect day.

Mr Hopkins seldom lost his temper, and this day perhaps his ailing wife had been particularly trying, but he was really irritated because my desk-mate had mischievously poked a hole through the bottom of her plimsole. We were giggling like a pair of loons. He called her out to the front of the class and as she hobbled across the spacious room he turned aside to hide a sly grin then tapped her lightly on the hand and sent her back to her place. He soon carried on with the geography lesson as though nothing had happened.

Mr Scriven (scrub) lived in the school house and taught history. The important dates were pasted all around the walls and were imprinted on our minds for all time. Battle of Crecy, Hastings and also signing of the Magna Carta. For our future information "Columbus sailed the ocean blue, in the year Fourteen Hundred and Ninety Two". Mr Maden a tall, strong, handsome man taught us beautiful poems and one from his own special collection called "Mamble" telling of the blossom-time in the leafy lanes of Worcestershire.

Mrs Edmunds gave sewing lessons and on the candy day of the week, pay-day, we were taught raffia-work. Quite intricate patterns were formed by her nimble, industrious fingers, she cleverly mastered the needle and raffia and by threading, plaiting and weaving turned the natural-coloured skeins of fibre into useful baskets and trays. Miss Adkins cared for the infants, also played the piano. She was, towards the end of December 1929, helped in the infants' class by a Miss Nan Mercer, who was a pretty, fair-haired girl.

There were two Miss Smiths. There came first, Miss Helen Smith, tall and willowy with a head of an unusual coloured hair. Some days in the sunlight strands of golden-colour shone through, but most days it appeared a burnished-copper auburn. As uncouth lads of our age usually did at that time, the lads in our class called her 'ginger'. A more refined, delicate creature would be hard to find. She was passionately fond of books, especially William Shakespeare, which was my favourite author thereby forming a friendly bond between us. Long after I left school she sent me a parcel of books also an informative letter on literature which I have followed up to this day and has helped me enormously in my own modest literary pursuits. Such a kind, unselfish gesture cannot be forgotten.

In the spring there were bluebells to gather for Mrs Malin, her gnarled hands betrayed the arduous tasks necessary to be carried out in a village hardware store. Our reward was a chunk of aniseed cake, usually tainted with a slight odour of paraffin, but we relished it with great gusto. This 'yellow peril' cake is not readily available now, but when it does occasionally appear, I buy a piece just as a sweet, nostalgic gesture, unfortunately there is something missing. It must be that unique paraffin flavour that only issued from Mrs Malin's kind, industrious hands.

There were trips from school to our favourite 'nature spot'. One such spot took us over the Alvechurch railway line, along the towpath along the canal near Shortwood tunnel. If we were lucky there could be a passing barge heading for Cadbury's factory when the 'boatie' would hand out a bag of unmade chocolate. In its raw state it looked like lumps of root ginger, but the taste was creamy and sweet: that was enough for healthy school children. Sometimes we could watch the 'boaties' pushing the boat through the tunnel by 'legging' it. This frightened the younger children for it seemed a dangerous practice as the men looked on the verge of falling in the dark evil-looking water.

We walked under the eerie, dripping aqueduct and eventually came to this little paradise of a spinney full of fluffy-tailed rabbits, moles, singing birds and the welcome sight of the carpet of azure-blue of the bluebells. Also cowslips, white and mauve violets (the white ones gave off this amazing scent) but the mauve ones were so pretty and grew so modestly beneath the moss-covered hazel trees. The spring sunshine picked out the delicate lemon-coloured primroses and gave an added warmth to the scene. This sparsley wooded area always reminded me of William Shakespeare's poem "I know a bank where the wild thyme grows"

The summer breezes and warmth seemed to bring everything into motion, the days seemed endless spent in playing cricket on Jessop's meadow. Although the game we played had no connection whatsoever with the real game played at Lords cricket ground by the experts. They did not have to contend with Ernie Gibbs our best bowler having to do his paper round, Ikey Curtis being called to have her tea or old Mr Faithful shouting "I'll scrag you young varmints if that ball goes into my ferret-pen again"

Gathering wild strawberries always attracted a few interested boys and girls. Armed with a clean jam jar we searched and searched for the scarlet jewels until the exulted cry was heard "I bags this spot". Some children picked privately and completely, intending to carry home the results to mother, but the more self-indulgent tasted the fruit to their heart's content defying anyone to call them greedy. It was very hard not to sample a few, because the singular flavour of a wild strawberry, especially if it is over-ripe and still warm from the summer sunshine is compared to the honey-sweet flesh of a vanilla-flavoured cherry.

Bank holidays, especially when the weather had been particularly hot, were a great joy. We would walk along the canal-side as far as Barnt Green and usually we would see the treasures half-hidden in the hedgerows − like a spate of golden coins, all colours, all sizes waiting for our devouring reaching hands. Beer bottles, pop bottles, and even unwanted fish. Some of those fishermen must have been rich. With the proceeds of the collection there was an unusual bout of heavy spending, gob stoppers, liquorice boot laces, sugar mice and monkey nuts. The "jeunesse doree" would flash around the chocolate trying to impress the girls.

November brought the excitement of Bonfire Night. We would scrounge all the cast-offs from the reluctant villagers. "That would do our Les another twelve month." Mrs Yeomans argued. It was always a battle to wrench any item at all from old Bella Howard. She would sit there by a very meagre fire-glow which showed up the very faded rose-patterned covering on the walls. After all the years the once-beautiful roses resembled smeared blood-stains, that was the comparison put forward by "Cocky Curtis". Making a signal for me to enter the cottage one day, she explained to me how to make "Kettle Broth". Such frugal living remained a mystery for there issued from "The Crown" a rumour that being a wealthy widow of a local needle manufacturer she could live in comparative luxury. She told me all you needed was a basin-full of boiling water, a few parsley sprigs, pepper and salt and a few crusts of bread. No talk then of meals-on-wheels, tinned custard or frozen chips. This mutual confidence filled me with a sad tenderness at the old lady's thrift, judging from the faded portrait over the fireplace she was once a lively teenager.

Bonfire Night came and went all to soon. The glorious colours of the Catherine Wheels, the Sparklers and the cruel fun experienced as the local ladies were seen to be avoiding the "bangers" that made them do a quick hop, skip and jump was all part of this autumnal feast. Although the seating arrangements were grossly uncomfortable not a thing escaped our notice as we munched our way through the dirty, undercooked potatoes and chestnuts ever alert and craning our necks everywhich way when the cries "Ooh! Aah!" rent the vaporised, misty, chilly November night. Tom Morris was always at hand to keep the logs and old mattresses well fired while Siss, his wife, kept us from hunger with slabs of cake and buns. The whole affair was well managed, finishing up with songs *Some talk of Alexander and some of Hercules, All by yourself in the moonlight* and *Love's old sweet song*, no doubt the words were changed after we had toddled home, and the brew had been passed around and around.

The dark evenings held no terrors for us. The game "Tag" pleased everyone until somebody's mother yelled "Bedtime" which spoiled the number. Some evenings we would walk a mile or so along the canal side to reach the affluent area to sing carols to the households of Aqueduct Lane. The group submerged all shyness and belted out the old favourites until mine host appeared with mince pies and hot drinks. Norman Whitby, the tallest, took charge of the proceeds and handled each individual share with all the dexterity of a Bank Manager.

Some Sundays a gentleman and his friend, I think I heard some one call our champion, Mr Greaves, after their Sunday morning walk would call in "The Crown" for a 'livener', but not before he had found the leader of the group of village children and entrusted him with a goodly sum to be shared equally. Simultaneously there was a throaty "Thank you, mister." In few minutes we were all standing on the step of Whitby's shop shouting "SHOP".

He was a man of firm intelligence, and smiled as each tousled head bent to examine his princely share out. This Sunday morning treat was something to anticipate with glee.

Mrs Wolfindale, featured a large nose with which she sniffed tremulously whenever her nerves distressed her, but a darling lady who massacred her well-tended cottage garden to present my mother with a bouquet. Sweet williams, canterbury bells, roses and my mother's favourite, mignonette. My Mother, always appreciative of a special kindness said "They are so sweetly pretty, God bless the two eyes that's looking at that woman."

Half way down the lane at the "Homestead" lived an old couple Mr and Mrs Warner. In their garden grew an unusual apple tree which produced a crop of the most honey-sweet apples. A penny worth of "Dodins" would last nearly all morning. Although the couple both appeared "scratchy" they manoeuvred my shopping bag so that every corner was filled to capacity. Mrs Warner was short-sighted and once, while I waited for my apples, she came towards the door, the local newspaper open in her hand and said "It says here 'They interviewed a suspected man who urinated from Birmingham'". Unbelievingly I glanced at the paper and smiled "No, Mrs Warner. It says 'originated' from Birmingham' ".

"My eyes ain't what they used to be," she said in excuse.

Children experience far more than grown-ups and the Withy Bed green crowd were no exception. We saw a Zeppelin plane fly over one day. It must have been in the 1920's. Standing on the canal bridge to get a better view there was much easing and shoving to watch the monster glide like a flag through the clouds. We were always at the heart of life and being naturally inquisitive nothing evolved or diminished without one of the group having direct access to the happening, also we heard rumours which were passed around about births, deaths or anyone leaving the district. We learned from an early age that nothing lasts, nothing stays unchanged, we could count on nothing. But at first signs of a change, we usually prolonged the extra bit of news by taking an indulgent ease while relating any particular news. When this happened someone would come out with: "I knows summat as you doon't know."

Bank holidays brought many strangers to the small hamlet. It was an exceptionally bright afternoon when we ambled along the canal tow path this day when we watched mesmerised as they pulled a drowning man from the greenish-brown water. The translucent blue of the poor man's face gave indication that he was well beyond any earthly assistance. The pumping of arms and heaving of chest exercises by Jim Skitt proved all to no avail. Graham Bassett said "Bloody big head. Tried to show off jumping off the bridge. But he got cramp." After several minutes of resuscitation the rescuers gave up and we walked away and, as though it was all part of the pattern of life, went off up Scarfeld Farm to collect chestnuts.

The air was heavy with the smell of meadowsweet and willow herb, the dragonfly skimmed the water, but there seemed a subdued quiet amongst us until Ikey Curtis shouted "Look, a kingfisher, there on that willow tree." To which we all gawped, and the spell of sadness disappeared. When I told my mother of the tragedy later on that night, she said, "God rest his soul. Some poor mother's son."

If you were lucky and hung around Batchelor's shop early enough on a Sunday morning you would have the task of taking Mr Batchelor's beer jug to the "Crown" public house to be filled for Sunday lunch. This being an enviable errand, for the reward was the run of the sweet counter as a "thank you." It needed careful timing, for if you were too early his wife would not have gone to church, but if you were too late his daughter Winifred would have already fetched it. As if from nowhere the rest of the late risers would put in an appearance and with ineffable charm enquire, "What yer doin' then?" just as you were about to have a quiet orgy on your own. But it was nice to have company and we offered a share, for it was an unspoken law that whoever made it to the shop first shared in the strictest sense.

The coming of Christmas struck magic, for the first treat was the school party. Miss James played carols loud and clear, and the joy of human compassion, being infectious, soon caught on and the old school timbers shook with the supreme volume of a band of happy voice The tables well-laden with the results of the village ladies' efforts: delicate sandwiches, rock cakes (Billy Goode said they were made from rocks), sponges, berry jams and the usual red jelly. Bill Ross said to Nan Mercer, "I'll have some of that," pointing to the jelly. "That's impolite," she said. "Well. I'll have a plate of impolite, please." The "Goodbye. Happy Christmas," was tendered with a "mystery" bag of wonderful "goodies". Apples, oranges, nuts, sugar mice and candy fish, in mine I once found a peculiar bean. It tasted like liquorice, but I've never seen or tasted one ever since and have often wondered if I had imagined it. But I still remember the taste distinctly. Apart from the seasonal bouts of sickness Christmas was a wonderful time, the family get-together, discussing the new addition to the family and sadly remembering the dear ones that had "Gorn on". I loved to be embraced by my Auntie Sophie because she smelled so lovely. To bury my face in the luxury of her uniquely-perfumed musquash fur coat brought a joy singular to all the old Christmas festivities.

We left Withy Bed Green with a sadness for the homely, rustic, genuine folk had shared so many precious moments with us. I long to pay tribute to their unstinting generosity and unwearying care when there was illness or hardship. Especially I see now the skill in the three dresses Mrs Beaver made for us three girls (my mother did not have a machine) for our dancing on May Day. I expect, darling, you are long gone, but nevertheless wherever you are I should imagine peacefully in heaven, may I say "Thank you."

There were so many treats. Tea with home-made damson jam under the plum tree in Bassett's garden. Home-made wine from Mrs Smith. Bramley apples from Dolly Yeoman's tree. Penny cakes from Pretty's Shop in the village. Singing hymns at chapel on Sunday nights with Selina Twitty. Sledging down Burman's hill. Skating on the canal. The kindness of Mr Whitby who forfeited our rent at Christmas.

Albert Brazier whistling on his way to work along the canal tow-path on his way to work at Austin's motor factory. Theodore Clifford and his pretty daughter Eileen. Mrs Edwards next door and Nancy Smith, who lived opposite and her brother Bill, a tall, gruff-voiced friendly boy. Marjorie Morris who lived along the canal, it was a well-known fact that she had a baby by a local farmer's son. They had been devoted to each other and courted for years, but as far as I remember they never married. On leaving I realised it was an end of an era. There have been many wonderous moments in my life, but in my rocking chair there will still remain those exquisite moments spent in Withy Bed Green and, more important, the gentle, modest folk who lived there.

My friend Mary

Miss Patience Rice

Haymaking at Scarfield

A Redditch family

A darling couple from Catshill

Patricia's family

Elisabeth II

Webheath
Celebrations
of Her Majesty's
Coronation

❧❦

Tuesday, 2nd June, 1953

Souvenir
Programme   6d. each

SPORTS SCHEDULE
for Wednesday, 3rd June, commencing 2.30 p.m.

2.30 p.m.	50 yds. Flat Race	Boys and Girls	5 years
2.35 ,,	,, ,, ,,	,, ,, ,,	6 ,,
2.40 ,,	,, ,, ,,	,, ,, ,, 7 and 8 ,,
2.45 ,,	,, ,, ,,	Boys	9 ,, 10 ,,
2.50 ,,	,, ,, ,,	Girls	9 ,, 10 ,,
2.55 ,,	100 yds. ,, ,,	Boys	11 — 13 ,,
3.00 ,,	,, ,, ,,	Girls	11 — 13 ,,
3.05 ,,	,, ,, ,,	Boys	14 and 15 ,,
3.10 ,,	,, ,, ,,	Girls	14 and 15 ,,
3.15 ,,	Sack Race	Boys	9 — 15 ,,
3.20 ,,	,, ,,	Girls	9 — 15 ,,
3.25 ,,	Three-Legged Race	Boys	9 — 15 ,,
3.30 ,,	,, ,,	Girls	9 — 15 ,,
3.35 ,,	Wheelbarrow Race	Boys	9 — 15 ,,
3.40 ,,	Potato Race	Girls	9 — 15 ,,
3.45 ,,	Egg and Spoon Race	Ladies	over 15 ,,
3.50 ,,	Three-Legged Race	Mixed Couples ,, 15 ,,
3.55 ,,	100 yds. Flat Race	Open	,, 15 ,,
4.00 ,,	100 ,, ,, ,,	Men	over 40 ,,
4.15 ,,	Final Event		
	Round the Boundary Race	Open to all ages

Events

CORONATION DAY, TUESDAY 2nd JUNE

9 a.m. *Short Religious Service*
at Village Hall
Conducted by Rev. T. Edwards, B.A., B.D.
(if wet, in St. Philip's Church)

6 p.m. *Judging House Decorations*
                1st   2nd   3rd
Prizes   15 - 10 - 5 -

6.30 p.m. *Fancy Dress Parade*
Assembly point—Corner of Heathfield Road and Hill Top
Class A—Best Fancy Dress, Girl
 ,, B— ,, ,, ,, Boy
 ,, C—Best Fancy Dressed Girl and bicycle or vehicle
 ,, D— ,, ,, ,, Boy ,,
 ,, E—Most Original Dress, Boy or Girl
 ,, F—Best Fancy Dress. Adults
 ,, G—Open, Adults
                      1st   2nd   3rd
Prizes — Children's Classes 7 6 5 - 3 6
         Adult Classes   15 - 10 - 5 -

Judges : —
Mrs. E. L. SEALEY   Mr. & Mrs. C. F. W. RENDLE
Mrs. E. A. COLLIER   Mr. & Mrs. C. E. GREENHILL
Mr. D. A. COATES   Mr. & Mrs. V. T. MOUNTFORD
Mr. E. POWELL   Mr. & Mrs. R. A. HODGE
Mr. & Mrs. W. ATACK Mr. & Mrs. L. LUDFORD

8.30 p.m. *Social Evening*
in the Village Hall
Light Refreshments   Admission Free

11 p.m. *Bonfire*
in Mr. G. Mills' Field
(Corner of Heathfield Road and Birchfield Road)

WEDNESDAY, 3rd JUNE

12.30 p.m. *Old People's Luncheon*
in the Village Hall
(For all people 65 years and over)

2.30 p.m. *Sports for all ages*
in Mr. A. Turner's Field, Heathfield Road
For details see back page

5 p.m. *Children's Tea*
in the Village Hall

All entries are strictly limited to residents
in Webheath and district as defined by
the Committee

*The Committee wish to thank all who have subscribed,
loaned fields and equipment, the judges, and all others
who have helped to make the celebrations possible.*

Chairman: Rev. T. EDWARDS, B.A., B.D.
Hon. Treasurer: Mr. G. MIDDLETON   Hon. Secretary: Mr. H. HUGHES

General Committee
Mrs. T. Edwards   Miss S. Boulton   Mr. J. James
Mrs. E. L. Sealey   Miss L. Fletcher   Mr. C. Powell
Mrs. A. C. Jarvis   Mr. W. Bailey   Mr. G. Tisdale
Mrs. V. Mountford   Mr. R. Farmer   Mr. R. Haden
Mrs. E. Boulton   Mr. G. Taylor   Mr. A. C. Jarvis
Mrs. A. Bryan   Mr. A. Drover   Mr. E. Boulton
Mrs. A. Clarke   Mr. S. Wall

THE ENTERPRISE PRINTING SERVICE, CHARLES STREET, REDDITCH

Impoverished by War

The first time I enjoyed a wage was as a paid house-girl to a local farmer's family. Receiving a handsome reward of five shillings per week, equivalent to fifty pence in today's coinage.

It was a very lively household, three girls and a boy. We spent long summer days romping through the apple orchard, after the house chores were completed. The gnarled trees provided many "hidey holes" and nesting places for many country birds. The orchard was at its prettiest about "Mothering Sunday" time, when the pale greens and shell-pinks of the blossom buds survived the greedy appetite of the bull-finch. Although the monetary reward was not great, the experience was, for the lady of the house gave me cookery and household tips that school education did not teach. Farm food is so nourishing. Even the plain supper proved to be a banquet. Like a simple ritual, Mrs Farmer would first display a real cottage loaf, a slab of cheese, home-churned butter and a massive jug of hot, milky cocoa. The "maister" made the same slow, deliberate movements every evening. Thin layer of butter spread over the "outsider" of the new loaf, then a chunk of cheese placed carefully on the top all washed down by the hot, chocolate drink. It was sheer "gutsy" pleasure to see this man enjoy the simple meal. One spring holiday there were visitors to the farm and I remember the industrious wife say everything on the table was home-produced, including the tangy, lemon-curd tarts. Although it took her nearly an hour to whip up the farm cream which today takes me two minutes in my Braun mixer. Boiled ham, salads, cakes, junkets. and paper-thin bread and butter. Mouth-watering thoughts of yesteryear.

My eldest sister had already met a local lad at church and every Sunday I was dragged past the village church where he "blew" the organ. There was an invitation for me to join them around the leafy Worcestershire lanes to act as chaperon most summer evenings. Although the walks were enjoyable I soon tired of playing "gooseberry". The first Easter at Webheath still remains a treasured memory. The boisterous winds of winter had died out and the distant Malvern Hills seemed to draw closer, as the violet shadows of stormy crags had taken on a new brightness, the greys and morose colours now were replaced by a pink and ochre sheen as it bathed the rough limestone on the slopes. There was a special feeling of a sixteen year old. I wore a silk pale-blue suit and some fashionable fawn shoes with a buckle that I had badgered my darling mother to buy me. The sudden rapture of new friends, new clothes and the sweetness of my mother's generosity signalled a new-born confidence that will be embedded in my heart for all time. Ray, my sister's boy friend taught us the names of local herbs, and flowers. We didn't chatter as youngsters do today, but strolled along in silence drinking in the warm, scented summer sunshine. The lad seemed to know all the hidden spots that sheltered the most wondrously scented, white violets, primroses and cowslips. He told us that he had asked his boss for a rise as he was thinking of getting married, but the boss told him "Well, Raymond, you don't expect me to keep the good lady."

My first real job was at Kays Ways Pays and, although the main thoroughfare of Redditch only boasted two main roads which crossed at the junction of Evesham Road and Market Place and connected with the Parade, a very impressive notice was placed outside the shop informing all and sundry that "Goods bought here will be guaranteed to be delivered to all parts of the city". Traffic lights were installed at this central junction about the 1930's. Straight down the hill to the left leading to the station is signed Unicorn Hill, which still branches off to the right as Bates Hill.

Population recorded in 1926 was 16,680. Inhabitable houses were 4,110. Rateable value of Urban District rated at £54,412.5s.9d. Near Prospect Road stood a popular fish and chip shop.

The proprietor sold cures for children's complaints. So the customer was able to buy 1d of chips and something for the baby's cough.

In Kays we were told to weigh the biscuits and then remove a couple to cover the stock. The hours were terribly long: eight-thirty until seven on week-nights and Friday eight o'clock and Saturdays nine o'clock. If we wanted to go to the pictures it was either Mondays or Thursdays (pay-day). There were many happenings at Kays and the staff were a grand crew. It consisted of Mr Jones and Miss Taylor and a very poorly-looking errand boy, who gave me a faint touch of nausea as he would take handfuls of raw lard and dip it in the sugar and relish this as sweet as a nut.

Perhaps the same professional competition still exists today, but it always seemed outrageous to me, when every Monday morning, Miss Marjorie Taylor and myself were given a long list by the manager which covered our main provision stock and told us to do a round of our competitors shops and ask for their up-to-date prices, so that we could undercut them. But for all the audacity of Mr Jones's method, we were never refused or rebuked. Perhaps they took pity on two silly, laughing girls.

Miss Taylor was a warm-hearted maiden with a gorgeous head of auburn coloured curls. She always reminded me of Jeanette MacDonald, a film star of that period. One day, "Kaka" our milkman, who delivered the milk in a large churn loaded onto a milk-float, was a rustic individual and had a crush on Miss Taylor. He would make any excuse to hang about if Madge was not serving in the shop. Usually she went out to give Neddy a biscuit, but this day the horse swung around too quickly and the shafts of the milk-float went through the shop window. Pandemonium reigned all morning among the high street shop-keepers, many shaking with internal laughter.

The prices at Kays then were: best Danish Tub butter, one shilling per pound (five pence) today. Best New Zealand butter eleven pence per pound. Good cheese sixpence per pound. Granulated sugar two pounds for three pence and a halfpenny. Biscuits five pence per pound. Tea three pence and a halfpenny per quarter pound packet. Streaky bacon two pence and a halfpenny per pound. My brother swore it was reclaimed from the sea after the great war. It was so salty. The better cuts of bacon such as the short-back were more expensive at eleven pence per pound. Some of our jam looked an unpleasant purple hue and looked like glorified, pulped potato. It sounded quite an impressive mixture from the misleading label: full-fruited apple and raspberry. Best country berry jam. Apple and strawberry, but it was a good buy at five pence per one pound pot. And a bonus of a penny back on the returned jar. Oranges were five for one shilling, very popular at Christmas. Lard two pence and a halfpenny per pound. Pink salmon five pence per medium-sized tin. Condensed milk was two pence and a half penny per large tin. I have often wondered what this was made from. Tiny packets of black-lead were one farthing as were also the neatly tied wrapped packets of blue. It seemed a "must" in those days to put in the final rinsing water of "whites" on washday a squeeze of the blue-bag.

People would crowd in on Friday nights from the outlying country side for their weekly orders. This proved a test of our mental capabilities for this had to be calculated item by item to produce the correct figure. The three farthings were the tricky ones, but after a while it became quite easy by sorting the awkwardly priced goods and assembling them as a unit, such as four bags of sugar at three pence and a halfpenny, and four bags of blue added up to one shilling and sixpence, and three bags of washing soda at three pounds for two pence made the level figure of two shillings.

Sometimes the manager would make a spot check and heaven help the one who was a farthing out. There were no recriminations if the total added to a few pence more. That will help balance the stock he would explain. Usually a truly rural crowd would come in on the country bus. One dear old lady took ages to make up her mind as to which luxury she could afford after the basic foods were placed before her on the counter.

Some weeks she would hum and har deciding eventually on a three pence halfpenny tin of pineapple chunks. But mostly it was, "I don't think I will indulge this week." Her husband being a farm labourer only received about thirty shillings per week.

We thought we were millionaires when we did find time to go to the Danilo Cinema on Unicorn Hill or the Gaumont Cinema in Church Road with a packet of Craven A and a one shilling ticket for the best seats. The early films of Janet Gaynor and Charles Farrell or Richard Tauber singing "You are my heart's delight" and later Leslie Howard in "Intermezzo", were our favourite films. Strutting around on our high heels and wearing the fashionable seamed stockings we imitated the glamour of the American casual style. I was walking down Evesham Street feeling like a million dollars, one sunny day, when my brother's friend said to him, "If that wench falls off them there high heels, her'll break her bloody neck."

On a date, the first thing we would buy would be some Californian Poppy scent and the new craze nylon stockings. They were so sheer and delicate giving already shapely legs a new attraction; we would give our high teeth and travel miles to obtain a pair. While they lasted Betty Grable would have envied our pride and swank.

Muskatt's Woods, beyond the town, along Bromsgrove Road always appealed to us, as it was quiet and romantic, and our footsteps headed that way more often than not. The Redditch Lover's Lane. A bench in the moonlight, a box of chocolates and a nice boy then all the world stood still for a few magic hours.

One lad's acceptable gift was a packet of Neopolitans and, when I see these dainty chocolates so finely wrapped today, the playful, teasing whisperings of that innocent rendezous dominates my thoughts.

The behaviour of the boys held no vestige of aggression or even curiosity. Perhaps they had been well and truly warned, for although in the summer we enjoyed our liberty a little longer, most evenings we were home by the fire by nine o'clock. We never anticipated much on these dates, just to be wrapped in the tenderness and innocence of youth, exchanging timid kisses and singing dreamy love-songs, quietly withdrawn as the approaching dusk heralded the end of romance for one night, we were content.

Will that pure sweetness ever return? I hope so, for there is something lacking in this ever so hygienic approach of today's lovers, the old thrills are well-spent before they really absorb each other's thoughts. We had the best of society, considering the ridiculous attitude of Victorian ideas, when it was the fashion to cover up the table legs in an effort to present a false sense of modesty. Now the pendulum has swung too far the opposite way. So we enjoyed the best, in those middle years. Perhaps it may have been the influence of the American films, for they did display heroism for the lads and an unreal sense of romance for the girls. But there must have been a hidden message for all, because the "goodies" always "got the girl" and as pure escapism every young girl had her "Errol Flyn". A quiet walk in a country lane on a warm, Spring evening with a decent boy was sheer bliss. A sensible courtship, then engagement and eventually the wedding. There is no substitute for love and if you have found it then you are the most heaven-favoured person on earth. And there are many such couples in Redditch, that has been proved by the happy Golden Wedding photographs issued from time to time in the Redditch Indicator. Good Luck and God Bless them all.

There were some strange happenings in Redditch at that time. Some poor soul had been given fourteen years in jail for stealing a gooseberry pudding, but I suppose that was relatively light compared with a labourer sentenced to death for stealing a pair of breeches. But that was in eighteen twenty three. They must have belonged to the Queen. Cyril Adkins started a coach service from Hewel Road which was very widely used, it was about nineteen hundred and twenty. I well remember the placard announcing trips to Weston-super-Mare for five shillings. Kinver Edge, Malvern Hills and Stourport-on-Severn cost but a few shillings. It proved to be a popular attraction for not many people owned private cars. It was about this time my brother Ernest decided to get some wheels and he bought a little Austin Seven for five pounds to give us youngsters trips around Bentley, Feckenham and if he was very "flush" as far as Stratford-upon-Avon. Petrol was only a few shillings a gallon and the maintenance of the vehicle my brothers tackled themselves; some efforts having had disastrous results. A leaky radiator was sealed by filling it with a can of rain-water in which had been thoroughly mixed a quantity of cow manure. It did the job perfectly, and all went well until the sun came out and the over-heated engine gave an unbearable "pong". Harry was supposed to have mended the brakes one night before going to fetch the fish and chips from "Smelly" Perkins. The four lads went out to try his workmanship by testing the brakes down Ivor Road. Harry slammed on the brakes — nothing happened. Before it gathered too much speed the lucky ones threw themselves out. The car fragmented before their eyes. Ern stayed with the car shaking his fist at the already crestfallen home mechanic. Harry said afterwards, "He's dedicated to self-sacrifice, I'm dedicated to self-preservation."

There was a well-known remedy for a puncture, replace the air with grass. This rapid repair has enabled us to reach home at Webheath many times. Also a broken fan belt may be replaced by an old stocking. Ernie asked Harry one day if there was any petrol in the spare can they carried. "Yes," said Harry, "It's five fourths full." Ern made a quick calculation and turned on him for being sarcastic. Boys will be boys and it was rumoured at the Rose and Crown that the lads sometimes did not wait for the fan belt to break before they pleaded with their pretty, blond passengers to remove their stockings. It seemed as good excuse as any to stop the car for a quick cuddle. Either that or they conveniently ran out of petrol.

When the Redditch Woolworth's had a fire late one summer all the girls were sporting fancy garters. It did not seem to matter that they were singed around the edges. They were fantastic colours and cheap, that's all that mattered.

Gladys, a friend of my brother, enjoyed telling me of the old days when they lived in a cottage in the woods at Ragley Hall. Apparently making a morning cup of tea was "murder". First the sticks laid and the coals placed carefully to hold the kettle. Then the continuous blowing of the embers to keep it glowing brightly until the steam issued from the spout. Sometimes when the water had not quite boiled the leaves would float on the top. "My dad used to go real mad and storm off to work on the land," Gladys said. She said there were many arguments, my dad would shout "This bloody stuff is smoked."

"I can't help it the lid doon't fit properly," my mom would shout back at him.

She said her mother would make a rabbit last the family of five for two days. One day it would be stuffed with a piece of fat bacon across its chest, and next day stewed with onions, carrots, celery and parsley dumplings. Gladys said "Her would walk with two children four miles to sell a few apples, plums and perhaps a duck. She would get about five shillings for the lot, and her hands were red with chaps and cuts when she got home. As we grew older life got a bit better, but I remember her saying when she lit the oil-lamp 'Now where did I put them matches, don't move for Christ's sake.' " At night-time Gladys said that one candle was placed on the landing to share between the two rooms. Poor Gladys had lost one eye while climbing an apple tree when she was quite small. But this never worried her, and when she was "made up" she looked as pretty as a picture. She often said "Tears never supplied any man's wants." She was full of fun and the store of jokes were endless. Some were true, but many, well, you made up your own mind. She had as much cheek as an elephant's bum.

She told us that their neighbour Bill every time he broke wind he kicked the dog. Poor dog.

Memory plays funny tricks and when I see a man with a dog-collar I think of Gladys. Her favourite joke was: "Mary Dors said to our vicar, 'Can we kiss here in church, vicar?' The vicar said, 'Oh, no, we shouldn't be doing this really.' " She died when she was seventy two, but she had a boundless sense of humour, and I miss her very much. Near to where Gladys lived there worked an old gent that sold coal and logs from an old horse and cart while leading his faithful horse around the houses he confided loudly to the horse "I'll bloody sell you if you don't behave. No, I doon't think I'll sell you today." Everyone smiled at old Billy Russell's arguments with his horse.

Hewel Grange men

Garden of Rememberance

Old style Politics

School garden, Alvechurch

A Redditch Soldier

Hewell Grange

My School friends

Bates Hill Church

Ipsley Court

Ernest Cater
My brother outside Old Rose and Crown, Webheath

Foxlydiate Nr Redditch

Working Days

About 1932 I was working at Piper's Penny Bazaar. It was a dark dismal place and the manageress was a Miss Yvonne Handley. My sister Minnie also worked there for a short while and as I only worked a few doors away at Montague Burton's my lunch hour was spent with the two of them laughing and singing and making stupid signs to the lads working opposite in Foster's drapers.

Poole's factory in Albert Street was a place where I experienced the benefit of a small wage. It was a boring job in the swivel room, I think the machine that I sat at was called the "rounding machine" which smoothed the heads of swivels. As an uninterested female I often wondered to what purpose these peculiar shaped objects were put to.

They were sized right from tiny minuscule to the largest about one inch long. They were made from several metals including a fine heavy brass which, when polished could have made a nice piece of costume jewellery. But I never envied the ground floor workers where the scouring and the grinding took place. One regular lad was called Jack Gilbert who courted Nellie Ralph, she worked in the swivel room twisting pins onto the swivels. They made a fine couple and were inseparable. She was always ready at lunch time to make his toast and a boiling hot drink. There also worked as a grinder in the floor shop a married man called Charlie who unfortunately had a soft spot for Winnie who worked with us. It was said that his wife "mangled" him when it finally got around the factory floor, it being a well-known saying that the wife is always the last to know.

Upstairs with us in the swivel room worked several local girls. Winnie Bourne who eventually married Ron Savery, the assistant foreman. Sadly one day I read in the Indicator that one of their children met an untimely death by scalding in a domestic accident.

Valerie Brooks was a quiet refined girl and I spent one beautiful Easter with her and her charming country family. They lived in a sweetly pretty farm cottage in an unadopted dirt road that ran off Windsor Road long before The High Duty Alloys had ever been thought of. After good home fare we took walks right to the back of Birmingham Road to where the woods began. Paths led us almost to Weight's Lane after bearing well to the left we eventually came out near Brockhill Lane not far from Batty's, the newsagent's shop. It proved to be one of the most carefree holidays I spent carrying our bundles of bluebells and primroses back to her appreciative mother.

The foreman over us girls was a Mr Brazier. A very popular girl was Nance Widdows from Beoley Road. Winnie Bourne knew how to dress and always looked smart in her black high heeled court shoes. Vera Poole made useful knitted bonnets in two tone colours. I wore my mauve and black for years.

The record at Woolworth's selling at that time was one of Bing Crosby's earliest called "Please", and we had friendly arguments as to who should go into the shop and say "Can I have the record 'Please' please." There was only one unpleasant accident that happened while I worked at Poole's. A girl was working merrily away on a rounding machine when she let out a scream. It seemed her long hair had become entangled with the moving spindle. It was a hospital job, but I do not believe there was any permanent scar. Apparently the guard had been removed for repairs, and in actual fact she should not have been using the machine at all, but being on 'piece work' and coming up to 'pudding week' she had decided to make the most of her time.

Friday was a good day. Pay day, and we all ordered our parcel of fish and chips. A filling meal for about threepence. We worked every Saturday morning and if it was not raining streams I walked home to Webheath which lay south of the town by about four miles. If I felt particularly brave I would take the 'short cut' up Bromsgrove Road and through Musketts Way. There were many worrying stories circulated from time to time about unsavoury characters skulking through the woods, and although there were never any frightening episodes I can recall, I was always happy and relieved to reach the middle gate where a few houses were dotted on the left hand side. After that the walking became more rapid until you reached the last bend where the bench stood, then you could see the ladies of Birchfield Road busy in their well-lit kitchens and the situation felt less 'hairy' as you sensed being nearly home. The fare on the local 'bus was only three pence return, but even this was not readily available some days. Towards the week-end I would be asking my brother John to lend me the fare. I can still see his well-bitten finger nails fumbling in his purse for a threepenny bit. My mother would say "What a performance, watch Brittania blink at the light." Those were the days and we were happy. We were a family and my darling mother was alive. She had the most wonderful sense of humour and even joked with us the day she was dying.

It was boring at Poole's factory and no great financial rewards, so I took a job at the hosiery works in Ipsley Street. This was a much bigger concern and all the factory rules were pinned up on the notice board for all to see. Proper rest room and medical facilities and also holiday pay. My job was to work the hosiery needle machine. The hosiery needles had a loose blade on the tip and placed in rows of a two dozen batch the machine worked the blades to and fro to ensure an easy regular movement a free working needle that knitted the stockings by mass production.

While at the Hosiery there was a girl there called Kathy Hall, a very homely country girl. She said that they had an American come to stay with them for a few days and the first day he enquired "Where's the bathroom, please?" She told him to go out of the backdoor, up the path, turn left and that he would see it under the damson tree. She said he laughed and repeated, "You don't understand honey. I want the bathroom." She said "I was most hurt. He wouldn't believe me. And I'd just done my lovely little lavatory out with a nice little oil lamp and a bit of carpet." He couldn't believe our toilet was right outside up the garden path. I suppose it did sound a bit archaic comparing their immaculate buildings."

Lady Eleanor gave a modern wireless permanent wave for five shillings. She worked from her house near the hospital. Lewis Beoley Road made faggots and peas. Customers left their jugs and basins every Thursday night on the step.

A local lady told me her sister-in-law collected butter from the Maypole shop and later made it up into half pound fancy rolls, forming a shape of a cow across the top and passed it off as pure farm butter to the unsuspecting locals. It seemed everyone raved about Mrs Morris's farm butter.

Mr Quinney was a councillor at that period.

Mr Fred Poole sold some factory 'shopping' to Mr Smith which started business as Woodfield factory. Mavis Bennett the famous soprano lived on Prospect Hill for a good many years.

There was an interesting story going around the town at that time of a pretty factory girl who had married a well-to-do estate agent who later became a baronet making the girl from Clarke's Yard a Lady. They became known as Lord and Lady Lambert. They enjoyed a long and happy married life and had three beautiful daughters, Anne, Pamela and Carol, the story always fascinated me.

Some girls from Heathfield Road worked at Pool's factory, some worked at Abel Morrel's making safety pins and all varieties of sewing needles. Also the Hosiery Needle Company in Ipsley Street employed much female labour. But, as I could not involve myself in machinery parts and things I could not understand, I settled my ideas on selling consumer goods which made more sense to me. I began counter work at

Peark's Stores in Evesham Street when Bertie Walford was manager and Charlie Heritage was first hand, Vic Ames was on the bacon counter. The quality of Peark's dairy goods were of a very good standard, also with the purchase of butter, tea and margarine the customer was given coupons which were exchanged for a very prettily patterned tea set. The full set consisted of six cups and saucers, six tea plates a bread and butter plate, sugar basin and cream jug and a handsome teapot. Only recently I saw this same patterned cup and saucer on a charity stall on the open market in Redditch. The long forgotten pattern brought back a wave of nostalgia, bringing back vivid memories of those far off days, watching the industrious ladies of Redditch carefully counting their coupons to see if they had enough for a prized cup and saucer, or whatever. Sid Bott was on the van. Goods were delivered to all around the country from the van and on returning the cry would go up "Check the van in". This was a welcome sound for it meant nearly time to go home. Early in the week we would go to the "pictures" to see the latest movie. Some of the ones I enjoyed were: French without Tears. Richard Tauber in "You are my Heart's Delight". Jeanette McDonald and Nelson Eddy "Maytime", "Desert Song". Janet Gaynor and Charles Farrel in "My Little Grey Home in the West".

On the corner of Evesham Street and the Market Place around 1932 stood the shoe shop owned by Huins. There worked there a very efficient sales girl Margot who courted Cyril Nash from Heaphy's in New Street. They were inseparable and eventually married and had a family who today control two busy concerns in Redditch. They made a handsome couple and are still a very popular, well respected family. Unfortunately Cyril passed away a few years ago.

Next to Huin's shop was Hodges, the newsagent's shop.

On the same side was Preedy's the tobacconist's. Then Boot's the chemist's. A lad I know said every time he went in there to buy a packet of unmentionables there was a lady serving so he said "I always finished up by buying a toothbrush." I asked him what happened when he took the girls out. "Oh," he said, "I took them behind the bushes and brushed their teeth".

Then came Murdoch's the tailors, and Miss Thomas's wool shop, and George Hopkins, the jeweller's on the corner of Evesham Street and New Street. The Maypole was on the opposite corner, then Rigby Davis, Hollington's took up a double space and sold most of everything needed for the home. I still have a complete set of saucepans bought from there during the war when household utensils were very hard to come by. Next door stood Tom Smith's the fruiterers and game dealers. At Christmas time this shop was a joy to behold, with the fine hares and pheasants hanging in rows, their beautiful feathers shining in the lamp light like spangles. The windows were adorned with luscious foreign fruits, dates, figs, oranges, bananas, melons, sweet grapes and nuts of every description from all parts of the world to be devoured by the good folk of Redditch.

Near there was Humphries's shoe shop. Dutch Court shoes were the fashion at that time and a pair of these complete with the fully-fashioned stockings with the seam running straight and level we felt like Betty Grable. Next came an old fashioned public house. It could have been called The Rising Sun, it closed down long before the new town began demolishing the area, and the shiny green tiles spelled the age of the building, after that was the wool and drapery shop. Mr and Mrs A. T. Turner were a very business like couple. The stock and shop were always in immaculate condition. And they were more especially liked because they were so obliging, and would always keep any particularly nice stockings or scarves for us girls that worked in the vicinity. They seemed to sense when we had a special date.

Then came Brown's, the corn and seed people. They also owned the yard that ran alongside. There was a great old character drove the horse and cart for Brown's. One day the boss came along and asked him where he had been the previous Saturday when he should have been working. "A better bloody job than this. I was cuddling my girl friend. Nothing in the world is better than that, gaffer."

"Oh, I agree Joshua, but do remember you also have a commitment to your employer."

"Ah, I suppose so."

There came past Brown's Yard a smallish shop and then Hollifields, the drapers. A tiny cooked meat shop lay back into the wall next door to the Hungry Man. A Mr Oscar Hewitt ran this public house with his goodly wife. Quite a popular and enterprising couple. My mother helped Mrs Hewitt and I called one day to give my mother a message and my mother opened the lift lid. Down on the ground floor Mrs Hewitt opened the lift shutter to send some plates up on the lift cupboard. My mother introduced us and as our eyes met down the lift shaft, my mother came out with, "This is Mrs Hewitt, my love. But she doesn't look quite the same upside down." I couldn't say anything to the lady for laughing. My mother's sense of humour was infectious.

At the top of Unicorn Hill there was a good class house furnishers Cranmore Simmonds. The shop itself set well back from the square, with large double fronted windows. Elsewhere in this record is stated the different prices for beds and other household items, and from memory I know one was able to purchase a superb three piece suite for under five pounds. Afterwards this property was leased by Sir Montague Burton who gave good value for money in their sale of bespoke gentlemen's suits for 45/-shillings. Also ready-to-wear for 35/-shillings. Also overcoats, raincoats and sports jackets and flannels. A subdued-coloured sports jacket and flannels really did something for a man. Before the jeans and tee-shirt brigade stepped in it was a sheer pleasure to step out with a guy dressed in that fashion. One date stands out clearly. It was a November night and the rendezvous was in Crumpfields Lane. I thought I arrived too late for, there being no sign of Romeo, I almost made a hasty retreat. Suddenly he stepped from the shadows of the arched trees into the lamplight. My heart missed a beat. He had on a dark overcoat and a white silk scarf, and with his black wavy hair looked the image of Robert Taylor. We had a wonderful evening. The moon came out later as we walked the Worcestershire country lanes. His name was George, but deeply sad to recall he died of wounds in France for he was called up for the army not long after that romantic interlude.

Coming back along the right hand side of Evesham Street, set back into the wall was a wet fish shop. Then De Grey's cake shop, beautiful sponges and fancy cakes. Morris's grocer's shop fine quality teas and dairy products. Jones, the double fronted shop sold ladies coats and dresses, blouses, and fancy boxed linens, socks and stockings. Between Jones and Moule's, the chemist, stood a small radio shop. Mr Moule had been long gone when first I went into the shop. When I knew it, it was owned by Mr Ray Shaw. He was a smart man, known locally as the poor girl's Errol Flyn. I did accept an invitation to traverse the Evesham Blossom Country with him. The Lenches were particularly refreshing that lovely May evening. I remarked how delightful the thatched cottages sprinkled with apple and plum blossom looked in the dappled sunlight. But all he said "They are full of fleas and liable to catch fire easily."

Why are men, especially English men so unromantic. Anyway he never showed the slightest interest in the spring blossoms or thatched cottages. It was made quite obvious that he had only 'one thing' on his mind, and now I've forgotten what that 'one thing' was. Poor man must have been terribly bored and frustrated, but I enjoyed the quiet pretty lanes and the fresh air. Something to be said for him, he did return my lovely silk navy hat bought especially for the uneventful date.

The Fountain was a good photographers, this was at the very bottom of front hill, and I still have many photographs of myself and my family recorded there. At the top of Front Hill was a useful tailor's shop, also a china shop but here near the Fountain was Maunton's the house furnishers, then a sweetshop, then a butcher's shop, managed by Eric Lakin. On the corner of George Street and Evesham Street was the large buildings of the Wholesale Cooperative Stores. Grocery, greengrocery, household items and furniture. There was a long queue every bonus day when the thrifty ladies collected their dividends.

From Huins shoe shop on the corner moving towards Red Lion Street, came The Regent, ladies coats and dresses. Sanders groceries, then Freeman, Hardy and Willis (manager, Dickie Gotobed), then the best Pork butchers shop in the Midlands, Marsh and Baxters (manager, Mr. Leslie Hales). One day when I worked there as cashier, Mr Miles one of the firm's directors, came in and saw Ron Humpage cutting out different chunks of shin from a half side of beef. He stood and looked at the hacked meat and said, "What are you making, Ron, a lantern?" Another time a member of the staff asked him if it was possible to have a rise in his wages as he was getting married. He looked very stern at the young man and said severely, "Well, young man. You don't expect me to keep the good lady, do you?"

They were wonderfully happy days. A top class strict manager and a carefree happy-go-lucky staff. On the window sales was Tom Dowding, he had the prettiest wife in the town, but unfortunately she died quite young from cancer. They had two lovely daughters. Second sales, Fred Saunders, Jack Trowman, Clive from Melen Street. George Harris, Alan Dyde, Arthur Hendley (Ben), Alan Harris, Bernard Rust, Stan Hart, who told me one day in town that not long after he had joined the Royal Navy "We were struck by a torpedo, but I remembered the drill and closed all the doors behind me. It was quite 'hairy' for a while. Worse than dealing with the gaffer, Leslie Hales on one of his bad days." Mr Hales made it known that he suffered from insomnia, no doubt the responsibility of the management of one of the most prosperous shops in Redditch. Soon after the Second War started he married a beautiful, willowy girl from Bromsgrove Road and probably this ended his sleepless nights for we never again heard him complain.

Bernard Rust was a well liked fellow with a great sense of humour. He had nick-names for all his customers. One wore a long black overcoat, muffled to the ears. "Here comes Dr Dolphus," he would mutter under his breath. Another poor man who suffered shell-shock from the Great War, used to put in his order and almost before Bernard could wrap it up he would grab it and quickly disappear. He was called 'snatch and grab'. Then the local factory girl who later became a Lady would come into the shop and arrogantly push forward saying, "I am Lady . . ." but Bernard would have none of this and one day he said to her, "I doon't care if you'm the Queen of Sheba. You waits your turn like all the rest. I used to go to school with you, if you forgets I doon't, so doon't come here with you airs and graces, madam." He did get into trouble over that one but undeterred he still had us all in stitches with his banter and ridicule. He married Marjorie Taylor, a local girl of gentle beauty and manners and had a long and happily married life. But one of the most tragic happenings took place one Christmas Day. Their only son, Michael motored into Redditch to pick up a Christmas present for his mother when he was involved in an accident near Studley and was killed. He was about 29 years old and a son to be proud of. This has to be one of the most poignant stories to relate. I often met Marjorie and Bernard at the graveside when visiting my own mother's grave. They had each other until Bernard died about 8 years after. Marjorie still carries bravely on writing meaningful poems and stories, they hold an understandable thread of sadness, but also some measure of thankfulness for the wonderful years they enjoyed, the three of them together, as she comes to terms with life's injustices.

After Marsh and Baxter's shop came Woolworth's sixpenny stores. They had a fire there and all the local girls sported fancy garters, it did not matter that there appeared to be a singed brown strip all around the edges, they were so glamorous, and the girls arrayed in every colour under the sun, gave the lucky boys the time of their lives for a few weeks. Next to Woolworth's Stores was a cafe where you could get a good meal for a shilling (5p today's coinage). Then there was the Royal Hotel then the Royal Hotel Yard were the traveller's winter quarters. The Clarkes, the Wilsons, the Chipperfields, the Harveys, the Henshaws, the Shufflebottoms, the Thomsons, the Hays, the Herberts. All good-living, industrious neighbours, and good citizens of Redditch. After the Royal Yard stood an imposing double fronted shop that catered for the more well-to-do of the town. It was Scott's, the clothiers and drapers. then a small greengrocer's shop, Hill's butcher's shop was next, set back, quite small, but in a prominent position and the meat was real farmhouse breeding, this always seemed a very prosperous business. It was later owned by Mr Jack Drew, a good butcher and very obliging and pleasant.

Then set a little closer to the road was Melen's jeweller's shop and then the Select Cinema. They called it "the flea pit", but it did improve as the years went by and they eventually advertised "all seats fully disinfected".

I remember seeing there *The Love Parade* with Jeanette McDonald and Maurice Chevalier. *The Desert Song.* Richard Tauber in *You are my Heart's Delight, The Student Prince* with the stirring, *The Vagabond King.* Charlie Chaplin where he ate his shoelaces, and eventually his whole pair of boots. It was hilarious.

Past the Select Cinema was Clarke's yard, there was a chip shop in that yard, also a few small houses. I remember Mary Ross and her sisters. A likeable lively bunch, lived in that area.

The fire station was in Red Lion Street, and later was used by Maxwell Jones, the sign writer, and there was a shop on the corner selling sweets and odds and ends. No wonder we were called a nation of small shopkeepers. Over the bottom of George Street was another little sweet shop. Then a few houses and a public house which brought us to Ipsley Street. On the other side of Red Lion Street was some factory shopping, and coming back to Alcester Street there were a few terraced houses and yet another sweet shop, which brought us to the three corner plot where once stood the old Police Station. I can remember a cottage being occupied on that triangular piece of ground and there was a path that took a short cut into Alcester Street. I believe a Ken Mallam lived there much earlier. Ken was kind enough to give me some details of old Redditch and being there he was in the thick of the 'goings on' in the town at that time. He tells of the open market when it was all along the side of the church in market place lit by acetylene lamps and you were in danger of getting singed if you got too close. There were many bargains on a Saturday night as there were no deep-freeze facilities to preserve the perishables, so everything had to go and the thrifty housewives of Redditch were' laughing' if they happened to live close to the town centre.

Next to Evesham Street in commerce came Alcester Street, a continuation of Church Green East. So, starting from the fountain end junction Easemore Road, there were the first three or four imposing houses that now are occupied by solicitors and estate agents. There was the butcher's shop owned later by Mr Fred Tomlin. His was a story of dedication and integrity for after beginning as the errand boy through years of loyalty, he eventually owned the business. He had a famous name for home-made sausages, even gave us the recipe, herbs and real pork minced meat, and my daughter who lives in North Carolina, America always insisted I delivered some of Mr Tomlin's famous sausages to America whenever I paid her a visit.

Past Tomlin's shop was Gold's the vetinerary surgeon's house. Mr Gold was well-known over a radius of thirty miles or more for his expert knowledge of animals. Recently this practice had moved to Astwood Bank, but over many, many years the only good vet around Redditch was Mr Gold. Behind these shops were a few terraced comfortable houses. I remember a Mrs Thornton living there. Her house was spotless with the snow white laundry smoothly ironed and airing on the metal guard, that served this dual purpose. The table neatly set for tea, with the firelight lighting up the fine cups and saucers. Tea time being a ritual, "the cup that cheers but does not inebriate" no tea bags, and the teapot warmed well before setting to 'draw'. Paper thin slices of real Hovis brown bread and butter with home-made jam. A banquet.

The Redditch Indicator had a gift shop in Church Green East, but before that was an old-fashioned draper's shop that boasted a circular staircase that led to the stockroom. The stock was so out of this world, fleecy-lined bloomers and corsets that had cotton laces to strap the garment together. Spencers was another item. I still do not know to this day to what purpose this peculiar garment was put to. I remember going in there with my mother, an old gentleman was serving. I always knew my mother to be an extremely modest lady and when he made himself available for service she asked him, "Have you any divided skirts, young man?" He must have seen me smirking for he made his way quite ceremoniously up the circular staircase and fetched his also staid and business like wife. Considering the hard-faced attitude of today's media sometimes I wish we were back in those sweet, old-fashioned days.

Near this shop was also a musician's shop, further along was a shop that sold tiles and fancy fire-irons. There was a hairdresser's run by Phylis Davis, a newsagent's run by Mr Wall and Lloyds Bank. On the corner of Peakman Street and Church Green East stood Webb's corn and seed merchant. Also they baked bread on the premises, there was a wonderful aroma down Peakman Street at baking times. These men began work at about four o'clock every morning. Like the postmen who began about the same time I suppose they eventually got used to the early rising which became a way of life, for they stayed in the job for years. In Peakman Street there was a fish and chip shop, The Sportsman's Arms, Webb's bakery, some dingy factories and St George's School. Off Peakman Street was Victoria Street and Wellington Street. There were many terraced houses built, no doubt, to house the many workers for the various factories springing up all around these side streets. Going back down Alcester Street on the left hand side was a shoe shop, Crook's greengrocery shop. Their salads direct from Studley college, were so fresh and crisp. Easter was an especially appreciated season for the lovely new potatoes, first rhubarb, and Evesham asparagus, such firm, delicious produce could guarantee a superb holiday fare for your festive table. I really enjoyed shopping in those days. Next came John Dyer's the hardware shop, this was a well established firm that sold lamp oil, candles and all household items.

Then comes Hedges the chemist's shop. There was once a dental practice near Hedges, a man called Mr Vincent. Next door was Popham's wool shop, a butcher's shop, Shakles fruit shop, Spencer's music shop and Canham's the wine shop. There was a public house here somewhere, perhaps The Rising Sun. There was a small draper's shop and at the junction of St George's Road was the Palace Theatre. Over St George's Road was the Liberal Club and the greengrocers shop, Mrs Davis. Next door was a smart cooked meat shop and then Mrs Thomas's butcher's shop. I think there was a timber yard next and high up some steps a sweet and vegetable shop then a radio shop. This brings us to the junction of Studley Road or maybe that area was called Pool Place, because I believe in front of Terry' factory there was once a type of village pond. On the opposite side of Alcester Street, was a tobacconists, then Marjorie Willis's dress shop. Mrs Marjorie Willis was my English teacher, sadly she died early last year, but Marjorie and Walter had a wondrously happy married life. Such a blessing on this earth. Next door Dolphin's chemist shop. A tiny wool shop, then Gailbraith's shoe shop. Mr and Mrs Gailbraith were a very happy couple and would chat about their happy week-end outings over the Ankerdine's. They had one daughter, Jean, a teacher.

After Gailbraith's, a dress shop, then a double fronted toy shop. The gentleman that kept this shop was a character. He always came out with some peculiar sayings, one day he said, "He who loses a cow and finds a horn, hasn't lost everything." I remember another of his quaint sayings, "To motivate anybody you have to be credible, to be credible you have to be consistent." Such profound things to say to a young housewife. After all I only went in to buy a few 'Sparklers' for my two boys. He was a bit strange, but he was only one among so many in Redditch at that time.

Jack Lewis was another character who worked at Terry's. He told me that his father had gone to the Bank (Astwood Bank) to fetch a sack of potatoes. Everything was alright until, on the way home back to Beoley Road, at the top of Back Hill he realised his brakes failed to function. This did not worry him overmuch as he thought when he reached the Alma Tavern the road would level out and he could peddle along comfortably. But this did not quite work out like that and he whizzed past the Alma, past The Warwick Arms, past the Kings Arms and right down towards Beoley Brook, where he eventually did stop. He and the sack of potatoes landed in the ford and got a real soak. And another day Jack and his father was gathering some wood from near the brook when two men came along the road from Birmingham (this was the old road into Birmingham) leading a horse and a loaded cart. The horse walked as far as the edge of the water where the brook had flooded, but would not budge another inch. Jack's father said "I'll have a word with him". He went over to the horse and coaxed and cajoled and said something in the animal's ear. This went on for two or three minutes when suddenly the horse moved slowly through the swollen brook like a lamb. Jack said he never told anybody what it was he had said to the horse. But whatever it was, it worked.

Another character was Monkey Law, the barber. Also one-armed

Danky. There was also Ernie Gibbs. His boss gave him the sack for being consistently drunk. The magistrate asked him why he was consistently drunk and he answered because he was consistently thirsty. Anyway when he told his mother who was as dim as her son, she said that it wasn't quite right. So he turned up for work the same as usual on the Monday and told the foreman, "Doon't you do that to me again there weren't half a bother in our house when I told me mam".

A factory girl told me that she worked one week so hard that her fingers were sore. The boss told her she had upset the rate-fixers programme and that he would have to knock off six pence from her wage. As she had to stay in lodgings because of the long hours she was given 7/6d per week to cover all her lodgings and expenses.

Another girl told me of the characters in Heathfield Road. There was Miss Bradley, never married, as it was said in true rustic village slang that she couldn't 'git' nor 'have'. This seemed a very peculiar saying. Mind you, it makes sense these days, where this deformity is more wide-spread than at first thought. One day I went into Mary's house and she grabbed a bundle quickly from the top of the tea pot. "Does yer want a cup of warm? Doon't mind these they be only me breeches keeping warm." On the sideboard she kept as an ornament a floral chamber pot. Inside the receptacle written on the bottom was: "Pick me up and use me well, and what I see I'll never tell". She told me many stories of the old days. It seemed Ron Humphries was the last working factory in Red Lion Street and that the Royal Enfield was built in 1906. Director, Mr F. Barry Smith.

She said a neighbour not very well-off asked one of the Brian's to decorate her front room. She had explained there was not a lot of cash flowing at the time. Anyway he did agree to do it. "You should have seen the bloody mess he made. You's never seen nothin' like it in all your born natural. He'd used up all the oddments he'd had left over from his other jobs, and said 'There that'll do yer for a bit.' The poor gel was nearly in tears. He was a bloody rogue, I'll tell yer."

She really stirred the villagers as these gossiping dirt brigade are apt to do, but she did have a mischievous sense of humour, and she could be forgiven this one natural fault. We worked together in a charity shop. In the shop we used a dressmaker's model to show off the clothes. Anyway, this piece of equipment was so delicately fitted together that once completed we were afraid to touch it lest it should disintegrate. This one morning we opened the shop door to find her in such a pathetic state. Her legs were haphazardly crossed, her torso was bent over a cardboard box. Her wig had fallen sideways, and her bald head lay unceremoniously near the fireplace. One hand fallen from her arm, as though she had really put up a fight, and the other hand seemed to be clutching a cricket bat. Mary took one look at her and said in her broad Redditch accent, "Gootel! What's happened to Frousty Freda? It looks as though her's bin on a tour of unbridled lust around Hemming's Entry. Her went to pieces in my hands yesterday I couldn't hold her and shouted for help, but there was only this shy young man in the shop. He said after a struggle, 'Oh, you'll have to leave it. I feel quite embarrassed, I don't like putting my hand inside a ladies skirt.' Big daft bugger, it was only a model, but he dropped everything and made a bolt for the back door".

Mr W. M. Moule ran a chemist shop in Evesham Street, not many stops along from Kays, grocers. But when I worked at Kays a Mr Raymond Shaw owned it. He was a dashing Romeo, we called him "the poor girls' Errol Flyn". While waiting for him to lock-up one night, as we were going out on a previously arranged "date", a customer came in for a packet of items and, as soon as he left the premises, 'Raymond quietly observed "He'll be back next week for a tonic." I couldn't grasp his meaning then, but I do now, seeing that we are recommended to take these items with us wherever we go. How times have changed.

There was Wingy Danks, the newspaper seller.

And the local gossip seemed to spin around the ladies: Fanny Fewtrel, Frousty Freada, Dirty Gerty and Vicky Sharp. Apparently they haunted Birmingham Road most evenings complete with white handbag, the badge of the trade.

Mr Lewis was the librarian and his pretty dark-haired daughter Belle, who was a beautiful violin player, made it a pleasure to go into the library, for she was such a refined, gentle creature, with a charming, friendly smile.

A few doors from Ellis's cafe on the Parade was the chemist Mr F. F. Bawcutt who displayed the old-fashioned phial of medicine in his window. Although the whole atmosphere of the shop needed modernising his made-up potions claimed to cure all ills. My mother had great faith in him and would take his advice in preference to the more qualified doctors.

A Mr Chamberlain told me that he bought a suit in the 1930's and he was still using it in 1982, still with the ticket in the pocket stating "If not satisfied, this garment will be replaced". In those days most tailors made a promotion gesture of enclosing two pairs of trousers with each bespoke order.

The "mad" barber at the top of Prospect Hill always gave his customers a bag of sweets for the children.

The open market in Market Place ran alongside the church, usually on Saturdays. It was well lit by acetaline lamps, unfortunately if the customer moved too close their hair was in danger of being singed. Saturday nights saw many late shoppers well after nine o'clock still striving for a last minute bargain.

An amazing variety of fish was available at Len's, the fried fish and chip shop in Peakman Street. Mr Chamberlain explained to me in detail the price of a good night out in Redditch in the early "thirties". He said, "We fetched a newly-baked loaf from Webb's opposite Len's Shop and put the fish and chips inside the parcel to keep warm. We had a good night out for a shilling, todays 5p Pictures 2d. Chocolate ½d. Fish and Chips 2d Cigarettes 2d and still had change. The cinema sold small packets of biscuits including a piece of Locust Bean for ½d. We also was able to buy homebrewed stout from a front room in Peakman Street for 2d per gallon".

During the war a local fellow took a small bus to Hewel Grange. "There goes the 'passion wagon'" the local lads remarked.

A girl I worked with said when they were 'hard up' they had 'spit-head pheasant' for dinner. I said, "My goodness, you must be wealthy". She laughed and said, "No. My dad was in the Navy and that's what they called Kippers.

When the second war started everyone possible was expected to work on goods necessary for the War effort, so most of the women folk went into factories. One of the girls, Gladys told of the palava in the tiny isolated cottage to make the morning tea on an open fire of sticks and coal. She often heard her father shouting, "This bloody stuff is smoked". "I can/t help it, the lid doon't fit properly," her mother would answer. She said she remembered her mother making a rabbit last two days for a familyof 6 people. She said, "Her stuffed one end of the rabbit with bread and sage and onions, put a piece of fat bacon on top and shoved it on the fire with onions, carrots and parsley dumplings mixed with beef suet. Bloody grand". She told us her mother thought nothing of taking two ducks, a few apple fallings and some plums four miles to the market. "And 'er 'ad two kids along oove 'er. All for five bob".

There was a Scottish lad who worked at Milwards called the canteen tea "White Inch Tea". He meant it was only a half-filled cup. Another short-sighted worker, Bob Jarret, was reading the newspaper to his mates. He read out aloud "Oh! Look, the cops have just interviewed a man for pinching a gooseberry pudding."

He read on to say there was a good cottage for sale with a sunken garden. "That usually means there is subsidence." said Nobby Clarke. "By the way how did you get on with Doris last night?" Bob answered in a melancholy voice, "Well, we went up Muskett's Way. We kissed and cuddled and leaving her at home would have been an anti-climax if there had been any climax to start with".

"Foiled again!" consoled Nobby.

The girl's talk was mostly of weddings. It appeared one Miss Brown was intending to marry Sidney Neasom and the other was going to marry Mr Thomas, the solicitor.

There was much gossip at that time of the Batson girls. In the family were five very beautiful girls, who first lived in Clarke's yard, then down Birmingham Road. I remember Carrie and Phylis, but it was Roma who married the prince. It seemed a well-known business man surrendered to the charms of this lively lass. She was a dark-haired stunning young woman. They did marry and eventually he came into a baronetcy when she became a Lady. There had been arranged a full course of house management at some finishing school which gave her the necessary polish to fit into the role and they had four handsome daughters. It was a fairy tale come true and had all the factories humming for months at the incredibility of it all.

When working at Kays Ways Pays it seemed the main trial of the month was stocktaking. Mr Jones, the manager, was in a sweat for days. I've realised since, if there should have been a shortfall, either in cash or stock for three consecutive balances the manager's job would be threatened. The staff at that time, about 1933, consisted of three "counter jumpers" as my mother called us and an errand boy and "Mischief" the cat. Miss Marjorie Taylor, or Madge, was first hand, myself and a young man called Roy. Miss Taylor looked like Jeanette McDonald, the screen idol of that era. She managed to expertly curl her lovely auburn hair into fashionable ringlets that fitted neatly across the back of her head. One spring day she came to work in a delicate pale-green tulle dress beneath the modest length peeped a pale-pink lacy petticoat. It seemed to me like an emblem of spring-time apple-blossom. She was, and still is, a vision of beauty with the prettiest mouth ever bestowed on a woman.

My first "perm" was given me by a Madam Eleanor who worked from her house at the top of Prospect Hill. It cost five shillings and was advertised as a wireless "perm", and it did keep the curly effect right up until the hair grew quite long, which is a better result than today's expensive hairdressing.

Melen Jewellers stood near the Select Cinema close to the junction of Market Place, Red Lion Street and Alcester Street. We were warned never to stand on the iron cellar grid beneath the shop window. It seemed the owner had nasty peeking habits. There was a time I remember going into that shop with the idea of buying one of the cheap wrist watches he advertised. But, in a sleazy way, he tried to demonstrate how elegant a fob watch would look on my chest. It seemed strange behaviour for a respectable married man. His wife was a stately, severe matron, very business-like, perhaps she was completely ignorant of this. In the town was an old coalman and while leading his horse around was often heard shouting at the poor thing, "I'll bloody well sell yer". And then almost within the same tone "No, I doon't think I'll sell yer today". It was plain for all to hear except this docile animal, who plodded with Billy Russell faithfully around the Redditch streets for years. Also another character who loved her horse was Ada Herbert. Her apparel which seemed more like a uniform, a pair of riding breeches and an old "gansy". Apparently she even slept "as standing" as the sailors say.

Down Unicorn Hill there was a good cooked meat shop as far removed from the modern "delicatessen" as one could imagine. Depending which day of the week it happened to be the steam-laden aromas emitting from the cook-house door spelled out the menu. Although the cow heels and tripe were a delicacy, it was the onion and liver mixture from the faggot broth and the smell of the pork-hocks gently stewing that made the pedestrians travelling up Unicorn Hill realise it must be nearly dinner-time, and soon the good folk of the "Tane" would be bringing their basins and enamel jugs to partake of this wholesome "grub".

It was well known this meat shop which went under the name of S. Williams, Tripe Shop, 46, Unicorn Hill. Ducrows had a "Hot" shop in Ipsley Street which sold mostly faggots and peas, black and white puddings and chawls.

Huins Shoe Shop, was on the corner, and next door E. A. Hodges the newsagents, stationers and toy emporium. Near Gordon's Arch stood a man with a wooden leg and when the local youths became obstreperous unscrewed his wooden leg and laid into them with it.

Redditch and surrounding areas were given a fine laundry service by the Redditch Steam Laundry situated in Bromsgrove Road and in Astwood Bank we had the Lavender Laundry. Thomas Ellis opened his cake shop on the Parade and also a cooked meat shop in Evesham Street. His Cornish pasties and delicious cooked meats were real food. The boiled hams were cooked on the premises and the pure fat covered ham coated in breadcrumbs was mouth watering. The Cornish pasties were "Real Food" and you ate it from the end as they do in Cornwall. First you bit through the shortcrust pastry jacket hitting the onion, then the gravied steak with its pepper, salt and parsley flavour. That was a meal in itself.

About that time in Redditch the main window-cleaner was Mr. L. Atkins. The chimney sweep was Mr Maine. Billposter was Mr Banes. The pig-sticker was Mr Pulley. Mr Birch sold blocks of salt cut to order.

Billy Hillman was Reds "F.C." and captain, who always played with his cap on. The team usually "changed" to play football at the Railway Public House (run by Sheltons) and rode to the ground in Red Lane in an open lorry.

Redditch Wednesday "F.C." captained by Fred Young (a butcher at Headless Cross) won both the League and Cup in the same season. 1932-33.

At that time it was Police Superintendent Smith, Sergeant Best and Detective Batche at the Redditch Police Station. D. C. Batche caught three persons charging them with sheep-stealing.

Neasom and White were the oldest established estate agents and auctioneers.

The old Fire Station was at the top of Park Road. The engine being drawn by two horses and the captain was Mr Harry Bough.

The old Council Offices were at Park Road and Front Hill.

The Smallwood Hospital which opened in May 1895 was founded through the generosity of Mr Edwin Smallwood and his brother William. Their goodwill has and still is, providing health and comfort to the appreciative people of Redditch.

Webb and Sons, the bakers, corn and seed merchants made and delivered the traditional cottage loaf and daily bakery items and flour. Delicious currant buns and cakes were sold for about one penny each.

The characters of that period were many. Charlie Field was one, he kept the scrap yard or "rag and bone yard" in Red Lion Street. When the old man "Charlie" died his son said, "Well, there's more room in the bed now". He was supposed to have gas-tarred his house through to kill the bugs, unfortunately for his neighbours they fled next door.

Also down in Alcester Street was a fruiterers shop kept by a lady of ample proportions, not a very gracious lady at the best of times. This day a lad from Terry's factory went in to buy some oranges which were in short supply. She flatly refused him. On leaving the shop he shouted for all to hear "Next time you does yer manglin' I hopes yer catches yer 'threepenny bits' in the rollers".

There was a very pretty young girl (it was a well known saying that the factory girls of Redditch were the prettiest in the country) always wore a very tight-fitting red dress They called her 'Body Ingles'. This name stuck to her for years.

Chipperfields Show 1908

● No, not the highest haysheaf in the world, just the bonfire built in 1902 in Bromsgrove to celebrate the coronation of Edward V11.

In Affectionate Remembrance of

SAMUEL THOMAS.

Local factory owner

Our Nell

Evesham St.

Pictures of quiet days in Redditch

The

Coronation

of

H. M. Queen Elizabeth II

CELEBRATIONS

at

HEADLESS CROSS

REDDITCH

on

JUNE 2nd, 1953

OFFICIALS

Chairman :
Mr. G. M. ANSTIS

Vice-Chairman :
Mr. E. W. NEWBOULD

Hon. Treasurer :　　　*Hon. Secretary :*
Mr. S. T. MAYNEORD　　Mr. EDWARD E. YOUNG

Committees :

FINANCE
Mr. H. Melley *(Chairman)*, Councillor A. Poole, Miss D. Melley *(Secretary)*
Misses E. Ledbury, J. Ralph, Mesdames A. Andrews, A. Huband, D. Lewis,
V. Melley, M. Willets, Messrs. H. Anderton, J. Clissett, A. Farr, E. Harris,
T. Lolley, S. T. Mayneord, E. W. Newbould, J. Newman, D. J. Pardy,
and E. Treadgold

ENTERTAINMENT OF ELDERLY PEOPLE
Coun. A. Poole *(Chairman)*, Coun. A. L. Davis, Mesdames A. E. Whitmore,
H. L. Anderton, L. Griffiths, A. Prewitt W. C. Newbould T. Normandale,
C. Treadgold and Mr. J. Clissett *(Secretary)*.

CHILDREN'S ENTERTAINMENT
Mr. G. M. Anstis *(Chairman)*,   Miss K. L. Harris *(Secretary)*,
Misses J. M. Thomas, E. M. Ledbury, L. M. White, Rev. E. L. Hickin,
Rev. H. E. Venables, Messrs. H. Melley, J. Arnold, C. Wigglesworth,
E. Harris, and I. Mutton.

ADULT'S ENTERTAINMENT
Coun. H. D. Spencer *(Chairman)*, Mrs. M. Willets, Messrs. W. C. Newbould,
L. G. Griffiths, W. A. Baylis, A. Morris, H. L. Anderton, D. E. Underhill,
R. Hartwell, W. F. Hemming and D. J. Pardy *(Secretary)*.

DECORATIONS
Mr. W. C. Newbould *(Chairman)*, Misses S. Mayneord and K. L. Harris,
Messrs. E. Treadgold, A. Farr, D. E. Underhill, T. Lolley, E. W. Newbould,
L. G. Griffiths and D. J. Pardy.

OX ROAST
Mr. W. F. Hemming *(Chairman)*, Coun. A. Poole, Messrs. D. T. Duggins,
J. Duggins, F. Young, T. Hawkeswood, F. A. Newbould, E. W. Newbould,
and F. Tomlin *(Secretary)*.

BONFIRE AND FIREWORK DISPLAY
Mr. J. Duggins *(Chairman)*, Mr. J. Humphries *(Secretary)*,
Messrs. A. E. Humphries, W. F. Hemming, I. Mutton, A. Morris,
D. T. Duggins, S. Wilkinson, A. Farr, F. A. Newbould, E. Harris,
and K. Harris.

CHURCH SERVICES
Rev. H. E. Venables and Rev. L. E. Hickin.

Thanks and appreciation are expressed to all unnamed helpers

Programmes 6d. each.

Programme

CHURCH SERVICES

8.00 a.m. HOLY COMMUNION
at St. Luke's and Methodist Churches

10.00 a.m. UNITED CHURCH SERVICE
Conducted by the Rev. H. E. Venables and the
Rev. L. E. Hickin, with the St. Luke's Choir, on
the Playing Fields
(In the event of wet weather, in St. Luke's Church)

1.00 p.m. OX ROAST
First slice will be cut by Councillor A. Poole

ENTERTAINMENT OF ELDERLY PEOPLE

1.00 p.m. LUNCHEON will be served at the
White Hart Hotel Assembly Room
and the Memorial Hall
ENTERTAINMENT will be provided by the
Women's Institute Drama Society

CHILDREN'S ENTERTAINMENT

2.00 p.m. FANCY DRESS COMPETITION
Children assemble in the Playground of Rectory
Road School
CLASS 1.   5 to 7 years of age
   " 2. " 8 " 11 " " "
   " 3. " 12 " 16 " " "
Prizes for 1st, 2nd and 3rd in each group and 4 special prizes

2.45 p.m. FANCY DRESS PARADE
Proceeding to the Playing Fields via Rectory Road

3.00 p.m. CHILDREN'S SPORTS
GROUP A. 12 to 16 years of age
   " B. 8 " 11 " " "
   " C. 5 " 7 " " "
   " D. Open event

4.30 p.m. PRESENTATION OF PRIZES
by MRS. E. E. YOUNG

5.30 p.m. CORONATION TEA PARTIES
Memorial Hall   Headless Cross Infants' School
Heath's Canteen   Methodist Schoolroom

ADULTS' ENTERTAINMENT

6.00 p.m. CRICKET COMPETITION and
TUG-OF-WAR COMPETITION FINALS
On the Playing Fields
Heats and Semi-Finals will take place
on June 1st, at 3 p.m. and 6 p.m.,
respectively.

7.00 p.m. TALENT COMPETITION, FINAL
On the Playing Fields
Heats and Semi-Finals will take place
on June 1st, at 7 p.m.
GROUP 1. Competitors under 7 years of age
   " 2.   "   over 7 and under 12 years
   " 3.   "   " 12 "   " 16   "
   " 4.   "   " 16 "   " 21   "
   " 5.   "   " 21 years of age
*Entries for the above event must be received
not later than Saturday, May 30th, and should
be handed to Mr. D. Pardy, 195 Evesham Road*

9.00 p.m. TRIBUTE OF LOYALTY TO HER
MAJESTY QUEEN ELIZABETH II
Led by Mr. G. M. Anstis,
Chairman of the Executive Committee

9.45 p.m. DANCING

10.30 p.m. FIRE WORK DISPLAY

11.00 p.m. BONFIRE
Both on the Wake Field beyond Chapel Street

GOD SAVE THE QUEEN

Souvenirs for Children under 5 years of age to be distributed on
Monday, June 1st, between 4 and 5 p.m., at the Memorial Hall

Sideshows and Refreshments on the Playing Fields

Prizes for two houses and two shops with the best decorations

Prizes for all sporting events

Neither Committees nor Officials can accept any responsibility for any accident or injury which may occur to any person attending any of these festivities
nor for any damage which may be caused to any property through the action
of any person attending the festivities.

The Enterprise Printing Service
Charles street, Headless Cross

Looking Back

Today my eyes travel over a much different landscape from the few country lanes left that run around the Worcestershire countryside. This is a wonderous vista of open fields. Here, deep in Devonshire, the biscuit coloured narrow road winds over the first slope down to the sea. The stillness and peace is ideal for writing. But there is not a day that passes that I do not visualise the old Redditch of many days gone by. When through Beoley Brook was the only way into Birmingham. When Holloway Lane was a tree covered arch way. When the only sounds in Evesham Street on an early afternoon was a couple of dogs having a scrap. I can imagine the Village Pool that lay near the bottom of Ipsley Street. I read through the names of people who lived at the addresses given in the old Redditch Indicators, and wonder what happened to them all. The old characters: Body Ingles, Tracky Hack, Kaka (The Milkman) Wingy Danks, poor "snatch and grab", Jack Pool, Charlie Field. His poor long suffering wife and their son, Billy Hillman. "Reds" FC and captain (always played with his cap on). The factory girl they called "Red hat, no drawers". Frowsty Freda. Such bitter sweet memories make my heart bleed.

I lived and worked in Redditch for nearly sixty years and I miss the friendly cups of tea. The reminiscences of the old times and prices. We get the good, the bad the indifferent, and it takes all sorts to make a world, but generally speaking the hearts of the Redditch people are in the right place. Spotlessly clean, honest and straightforward. They tend to call a spade, a spade, but that is no great fault. Also they have a dry sense of humour. The first time I went to Spain, I was having difficulty finding the 'loo', I had an accident with my reading glasses and was not in the best of tempers when out of the crowded waiting room I heard the unmistakeable accent "Where be you going, kid?" It was a near neighbour and I was never so thrilled to see anyone so much in all my life.

*a Sweet Mystery of Life "Goodbye" From White Horse Inn, Donkey Serenade

Among my thoughts will be the care-free factory girls singing at their benches* "Loves Old Sweet Song", "Maid Of The Mountains", "When I'm Calling You", "Have You Ever Been Lonely?", "All By Yourself In

The Moonlight", "Moonlight And Roses", "Goodnight Sweetheart", "My Little Grey Home In The West", "My Old Dutch", "The Bells Are Ringing For Me And My Gal", "When The BLue Of The Night Meets The Gold Of The Day", "When Irish Eyes Are Smiling".

I kept a cafe in Redditch for quite a while and often think of the youngsters who helped me. Doris, Beverly Bant, Millie Brough, Stanley Blackford, Lona, Philip. One lad, I asked him to come to the Christmas party, he answered quickly, "Oh no. I can't get hissed on a Thursday". I answered quite politely, "I see. Perhaps another day". They were all good lads and lassies. We had great fun sorting out the juke box and deciding which new record was "top of the pops". "I can't stand that wench screaming her threepenny bits off" John Brough always said whenever anyone played Cilla Black's record, and he disappeared every time she started the first top notes of "Anyone Who Had A Heart".

It was the start of the Beetles craze and I could not understand what all the fuss was about, but now, I feel ten years younger when I hear again "I'm shakin' a baby now, twist and shout, twist and shout". I suppose it was the sheer joy of living. The Beetles made life worth living and my young customers loved all their songs. They really livened things up in my cafe. "Yellow Submarine". "She Loves You Yeah, Yeah, Yeah. With A Love Like That You Know It Can't Be Bad". There were also many other jolly records. Dave Clarke's "Bits And Pieces", "Telstar", "Silence Is Golden", "I Was Only 24 hours From Tulsa, Only One Day Away From Your Arms", "Great Balls of Fire". "I hear the sound of distant drums". "Blue Bayou" and of course Jim Reeves who pleased the courting couples with his "Put Your Sweet Lips A Little Closer To The Phone, Just Pretend That We're Together All Alone".

A few other names I remember: Ray from Studley, Bob and Mary from Sillins Avenue, Kenny Brough, he was always helpful and one day went all the way to Birmingham to get me a spare part for the juke box. Paddy, George, Nobby Clarke, Gordon, Philip, Emmy, Linda, Barbara. One weekend the boys went away to camp and the girls were left at home to play all the sad songs on the juke box, until Doris said "Big Girls Don't Cry" some other songs in fashion: "I Wanna Be Bobbie's Girl", "Bo Didley".

"Just Like Eddie", "There was I a walking down the street singing Doo wa diddie diddie doo wa di day. She looks good, She looks fine, Soon I'll know that she'll be mine", "I just wanna stay here and love you", "I'm into something good", Lulu sang a loud song "Shout", Seekers "The Carnival is Over", Sandie Shaw in bare feet sang "Puppet on a String", Cilla Black sang "Anyone Who Had A Heart", Petula Clarke sang "Down Town", "Walking Back to Happiness", Val Doonican sang a beautiful song, "I Chase the Bright Elusive Butterfly of Love" and an unknown singer came up with a pretty song, "We'll go on a Journey, Just You and I. To a place no one knows and that's how it goes, When we're alone we will make love". He never made another song at all. There was another song "Where do you go to my lovely?" and the well known comedy one by Sophie Loren and Peter Sellars "Oh, doctor I'm in trouble, my heart goes bumpity bumpity bump, every time he looks at me". There was Kenny Ball (just a minute) "When you Smile".

I miss the handsome cherry blossom tree in the churchyard shaped like an umbrella, also the well laid out beds of spring flowers, expertly designed for shape and foliage. It was pleasant to enjoy the fitful sunshine on a spring day on the church bench near the portals of the town church, St Stephen's, and think of the members of my family who have been christened, married or buried from there.

In summer the pleasure of walking over the meadows near the Beoley Paper Mills towards the church of St Leonard's at Beoley, and the lanes around Ipsley Church before the new town filled the area with houses, even down Watery Lane with not a motorway in sight.

Autumn also had its beauty, such as seeing the collection of different trees there in Musckettes Way when this sad season turned the whole area into a mound of bright coloured wine gums. The ferns still and damp glad, no doubt, of the winter's rest to come, but yet sending out some message to blend with the brownish mood of spent leaves and falling acorns.

And 'if winter comes, can spring be far behind'. Many times I visualise the black whistling ducks still waddling over the ice under the bare willow trees on Batchley pond in the heart of the winter, and taking my children by the hand when they were young to feed the poor frozen birds that gathered around like a sprinkling of coloured beads.

In winter the thought of the modern precinct dressed for Christmas gives a warm family glow, for the managers of the Kingfisher Centre really go to town and, as mature as I am, there is a childish thrill in the snow covered models and winter chariots all laid out to promote commerce. From afar I can only wish these smart modern shops and arcades full of smart modern people all the luck and prosperity in the world, but deep down, my thoughts and joy is in the old Market Town of Evesham Street and over past the church down Prospect Hill (Fish Hill) and Alcester Street and Unicorn Hill Crossroads peopled by the friendly banter "How's commerce today?" or the shoppers on the green gossiping "Well. Does you know, kid?". "No". "Well. See them two over theer. Doon't look nay, but they ain't got to yapnees to rub together. All kippers and curtains".

It's obscene to eavesdrop but I will not be completely happy until I can hear again the meaningless tirade in that Redditch accent that spells home to me no matter where on earth I may be.

By the middle of the eighteenth century the population of Webheath and Tardebigge had increased by the development of the needle industry. Messrs Milward's firm was founded in 1730 and it was said that some four hundred people in Redditch were engaged in some form of needle manufacture. Many of the ladies of Redditch were given work to complete in their own homes, such as the light furnishing and fancy packing of the many hundreds of different types of sewing and surgical needles. Redditch was smaller than Tardebigge but now we have a town of nearly 80,000 inhabitants. There have been many fortunes won and lost in Redditch. The 1939 war brought many losses to the mothers of Redditch. I am glad to say all my family returned safely from foreign parts where they went to fight the fight. Although my brother John could never quite understand why British soldiers always had to fight and defend their country from such dreadful foreign parts. He said that he would willingly stand in Heathfield Road with a gun to defend his own house. But why Africa, India, Egypt, Sudan and many other places he had only seen on a map. He remembered an American saying to him when they met some British soldiers miles from anywhere on this tiny island, it could have been Belize "What brings the British right down here?" Anyway wartime in Redditch was fairly quiet except the night of the Coventry blitz. It was a brilliant moonlit night and soon we heard the frightening deep drone of the aeroplanes from Germany. My mother used to say "The B's are back again." I was expecting our first son. And I remember my brother saying, "If ever that child survives it will be a miracle." We went over the meadows at the back of Heathfield Road and watched the planes going over in droves. There were some incenderies dropped on The High Duty Alloys and before the night was out from Webheath we could see the night sky over Coventry scarlet with the flames of war. Also there was a direct hit on some houses down Back Hill and I believe a lady and her husband were casualties. There were no groceries to be bought only on ration books. I even dreamed one night I could hear the rustle of onion skins, I think I missed the onion more than anything. The dried egg was good, but if overcooked tasted like rubber. It seems incredible now that we had only one pot of jam to last a month. The best item I found was the tins of sausage meat the Americans sent over. The contents described on the tin seemed quite dull, but the sausage meat was so highly spiced that gave our jaded palates just the right taste. The pork fat that lined the tin was an added bonus. I stuffed a marrow with this super filling and with the delicious lard made an apple pie. We had a banquet for a few shillings. Never since then has this commodity appeared on our shelves. One pleasant memory of those dark and dismal days. My mother's prayers were answered when all my brothers returned home safely from the war and we had to piece our lives together again. I well remember the plane going over Abbeydale giving the Victory V sign on 'D' day and put my hands together in thanksgiving. My eldest son, David, was five, my second son Terry was three and Cynthia was a baby. Now we all have to prepare ourselves for the "greenhouse effect" which, if what the scientists tell us is to be believed, the waters will rise up and Redditch could be a seaside resort. I cannot imagine bathing in the sea down where Beoley Brook once flooded its banks. But that is in the future and until then I have a lot of living to do.

Evesham St. Redditch

Redditch in Nineteen Seventeen

There stood a fine shop at five, Evesham Street, Redditch called Grays. The central cigar store. They also made picture frames.

The Liverpool and London and Globe Insurance Company advertised total assets to exceed fourteen million pounds. They had agents A. E. Hill, Easemore Road, A. O'Neal, thirty seven, Glover Street, B. Perrins, Evesham Street, W. G. Facer, Evesham Road, Alcester, J. Lewis, Feckenham, J. Richmond, Oldberrow, W. Jone, Hill Farm, Henley-in-Arden, John Hill, High Street, Studley.

The Needle District Almanac was in its fifty ninth year, published by the Redditch Indicator Limited.

Household coke was on sale delivered by the Redditch Gas Company. "Household coke one and sixpence per bag" Orders taken at eighty nine Evesham Street or direct from the Gas Works.

The population in the Parish in one thousand, eight hundred and sixty one was five thousand five hundred forty one. Mr Avery in his charming book claimed that in the year eighteen hundred his birth brought the total population to one thousand, that made the total in that year .

Eighteen Hundred and Seventy One the population numbered six thousand, seven hundred and thirty seven.

Eighteen hundred and eighty one it went up to seven thousand five hundred and eighty seven, and in eighteen hundred and ninety one it numbered eight thousand, two hundred and twenty seven.

Urban Council District in eighteen hundred and ninety one the good people of Redditch numbered eleven thousand, three hundred and eleven.

Nineteen hundred and one was registered at thirteen thousand, four hundred and ninety three, and in the year nineteen hundred and eleven. There were fifteen thousand, four hundred and sixty three. Inhabitable Houses numbered in nineteen hundred and eleven: Three thousand, seven hundred and fifty.

The Urban District Council met at six p.m. on the first Tuesday of the month at the Council House, Evesham Street.

Chairman: Edward Thomas Moule, Lineholt, Oakley Road.

Vice Chairman: Jesse Guise, Salop Road.

At thirty one Evesham Street was Scorza and Oliver, managed by A. H. Chatterley, Wines and Spirits, Ales and Guiness Stout.

At the railway approach was H. Wilkes, Tobacconist, Newsagent and Circulating Library.

John Morris, Ceylon and Indian Tea Store, Evesham Street.

Webb and Sons advertised Hungarian, American and Finest English Flour.

Fish Hill House sold ales and stouts in casks and bottles.

Private Schools

There was Grafton House School, Worcester Road. Principal: Miss Grose and Miss Bryant.

Kindergarten School. Miss Heaphy, New Street.

Osborne House School: Principal: Miss Harbon.

St Louis School. The Poplars, Beoly, care of Sisters of St Louis.

The Smallwood Hospital opened twenty fifth May, eighteen hundred and ninety five. Founded by Edwin and brother William Smallwood. Number of beds sixteen and four cots for children. Qualifications for governor was subscription of one guinea.

Uncle John's Cottages. Beoley Rd, Redditch

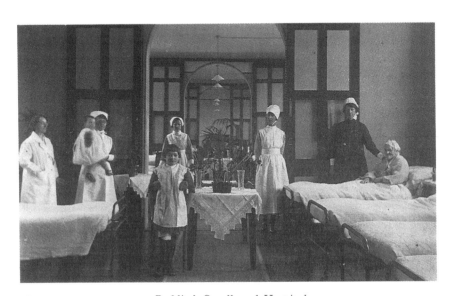

Redditch Smallwood Hospital

Muscatt's Way, Redditch

Evesham Road, Headless Cross

Church Green, West Redditch

Redditch Football Team

Webheath St Philips Football Club 1914

Redditch Football Club

"The Village Inn,"

BEOLEY,

Near REDDITCH.

GILBERT TOWERS,

Proprietor.

THE MIDLAND COUNTIES HERALD, LTD., BIRMINGHAM.

GILBERT TOWERS, Proprietor.

Churches & Institutes

St Stephen's Church was erected in 1854/5 at a cost of £7463. Bordesley Abbey founded by Empress Maud, daughter of Henry 1st in 1138 for Monks of the Cistercian (Monks) Order. It was dedicated to the Blessed Virgin. The charter was confirmed by Henry 2nd, Richard 1st and Edward 1st. The monastery is supposed to have covered 8 acres of land. A chapel was left standing at demolition of monastery and appropriated to the celebration of worship of the Church of England in 1688 which was continued until 1806 up to which time it was the only place of worship for the inhabitants of the town. On the surrender of the Abbey in 1539 by John Dey, the last Abbot, the lands were given by Henry VIII to Lord Windsor in exchange for the Manor of Stanwell near Windsor. Excavations made by Captain Bartleet by permission of Baroness of Windsor revealed relics, some splendid encaustic tiles now laid down in the vestry of St Stephen's Church.

Mr Polyearp Allcock first situated at the top of Unicorn Hill but when he moved to Clive Road about 1800 the factory was classed as the world's largest fishing tackle manufacturer.

The Enfield Cycle Company (The Royal Enfield Cycle and Motor Cycle Manufacturer) was first opened in Hunt End, the founders being Mr Albert Eadie and Mr Robert Walker Smith (managing director) started in 1892. Royal Enfield began to work from Hewel Road in 1907. Their slogan stated "Made like a gun".

We saw the first Motor Cycle 2¼ h.p. in 1900 and later the Royal Enfield two stroke. Two and three quarter h.p. The solo machine the 8 h.p. RE side-car combination came a little later on.

At the Select Cinema you were allowed to sit at the front of the stage on a mat for the price of 2d. A girl friend told me when the film "Sonny Boy" was shown she cried her eyes out all through the show and when she went home her mother said "Enjoying yourself, indeed. You look as if you have been dragged through the hedge backwards."

There was available for the poorer families a charity that provided free boots for the boys and Ray Smith said when the soles wore out his father replaced the soles with machine-webbing from the "throw-outs" at the factory, but he painfully recalled that this webbing was so rigid that it was impossible to manipulate the feet properly when walking so, he had the appearance of a duck's ungainly waddle.

The Redditch Indicator published twenty four words for one shilling forty five p.m., eight p.m. Beaufort Street. W.B., Beoley Road. T.S.O., Bredon. W.B., Bromsgrove Road W.B., Easemore Road. W.B., Evesham Street. T.S.O., Hewell Road. W.B., Ipsley Green. P.B., Littleworth. W.B., Lower Green. P.B., Mount Pleasant. T.S.O., Oakley Road (lamp box). Oswold Street. W.B., Prospect Hill. W.B., Unicorn Hill. P.B.

P.B. Traders: Edward Dyer. Auctioneer, valuer, estate agent, accountant, twenty two, Church Green East. Charles Hughes and Son, the popular furnishers. Evesham Street Stores. Glass, china, fancy goods. Indicator fancy goods department (whist drivers, etc), four, Prospect Hill. Willetts Bros. English meat, sausages, beef and pork, eighteen, Evesham Street, Redditch. F. P. Dolphin. Prize dairy butters, margarine, eggs and lard. Sturges. W. J. Scrap iron. Rubber waste. Skins. The Scrap Stores, Peakman Street. Postal Address: Twenty, Mount Pleasant. Mark Johnson, Church Road, wreaths and bouquets. Landcape gardening by season or otherwise. Saturday market stall. Number five or Nurseries Church Road and Easemore Road. Harry B. Tarleton, Ipsley Street. Shop fitting. Royal Enfield. Agent. A. Bell and Company, Market Place. Cycle and motor cycles. Thirty models. Two and a quarter horse-power, three horse-power and six horse-power.

At that time there was no Plymouth Road. That area was called the Soudan leading off from Cemetery Lane. There was no Batchley Estate or Abbeydale Estate. Some of the central streets were called: Glover Street, Mount Street off Marsden Road, Union Street, Lodge Road, Milsborough Road, Summer Street off Mount Pleasant, Ipsley Street, Beoley Road, Salop Road, Ludlow Road, Oakley Road, Evesham Street, George Street, Red lion Street, Grove Street, Alcester Street, Church Green West, Church Green East, Market Place, Union Street, Victoria Street, Wellington Street, Archer Road, Other Road, Peakman Street, Walford Street, Park Road, Littleworth, Worcester Road, Prospect Hill, New Street, Birmingham Road, Unicorn Hill, Hall Street (off Unicorn Hill), Bates Hill, William Street, Church Road, Hewell Road, Windsor Street, Melen Street, Clive Road, Brockhill Lane, Albert Street (off Prospect Hill or Fish Hill), Cemetery Road, Parsons Road (off Mount Pleasant). Bromsgrove Road and off there was the leafy wooded walk called "Musketts Way". Beoley Road, Prospect Road, Arrow Road, Off Front Hill a yard called "St Catherine's Place" a bit further up the hill on the left was "Izod's Yard". Hemming's Entry was nearer the town centre. There was the well-known "Back Hill" and "Front Hill", Ivor Road, Holloway Lane, Studley Road, Silver Street, St George's Road, Grange Road near St George's Church, Queen Street off Alcester Street, West Avenue, New Street off Walford Street into the main Evesham Street, Smith Street off Alcester Street into Wellington Street, South

St. Stephens Church - Redditch

based on a coloured lithograph, circa 1890

Street, Oswold Street, Orchard Street, Beaufort Street, Clive Avenue off Clive Road, Summer Street off Lodge Road, Britten Street, Edward Street, Bridge Street.

Governing Bodies: County Court. Burial Board. Rate Collectors. Town Crier: T. Marshall, seven, Peakman Street. Officer of Customs and O.A.P. Officer. Income Tax officials. Inspectors of Weights and Measures: E. poulson, four, South Crescent, Bromsgrove. Factories and Workshops: F. G. Mudford. Thirty eight, Foregate Street, Worcester. United States Consular Agency: William. U. Brewer, Unicorn Hill. Perpetual Commissioners. Public Schools. Redditch District Education Committee. Alderman. G. W. Hobson (chairman). Redditch Higher Education Committee: Mr F. C. Dolphin, J.P. (chairman). Secondary School principal: W. Rigby. B.A.B.Sc. Senior Mistress: M. Stirling. Clerk: C. E. Knight, forty seven, South Street.   Technical School: Easemore Road. Foundation stone laid by the Right Hon. Earl of Plymouth. November, eighteen ninety nine. School of Art. Church Road. Headmaster: Mr E. Lupton Allen A.B.C.A. St Stephen's Schools: Peakman Street. Boys' Headmaster: Mr E. T. Moule. Girls' Head Mistress: Miss Oakton. Infants' Head Mistress: Miss Brideoake. St George's Schools, St George's Road. Mount Carmel School, Beoley Road. Redditch Grouped Schools. St Luke's School, Headless Cross.

Redditch Institute, Church Road. Founded eighteen fifty. Small wood almshouses. Opened June, twenty second, eighteen ninety seven. Places of Worship: St Stephen's Church. Communicants' Guild. Women's Bible class. Clergy: The Rev. J. M. Short, twenty two, Bromsgrove Road. Churchwardens: Mr E. T. Moule, "Lineholt", Oakley Road. Mr H. A. Pearson. Old Bank House. Organist: Mr J. R. Reeve. F.R.C.O. Bromsgrove Road. Acting Clerk then: Mr S. Hawkins, Sheldon Cottages, Ipsley Street. Sunday Schools: Boys and Girls. Ten Thirty a.m. and Two Thirty p.m. Infants: Eleven a.m. and two thirty p.m. Mothers' Meeting at George Street Mission Room. Band of Hope and King's Messengers at Church Institute Mondays. King's Messengers (Senior) Girls: Thursdays, seven thirty. Church Institute. Sunday School Clothing Club. Payments taken every Sunday. St George's Church: Vicar: Rev. G. L. Michell. M.A. Twenty six, Beoley Road. Churchwardens: Mr H. T. Milward and Mr H. Fourt. Organist: Mr E. Parsons, Bromsgrove Road. Acting Clerk then Mr C. Chambers, thirty three, Other Road. St George's Sunday School ten thirty a.m. and two thirty p.m. St George's guilds. Senior and Junior. Church Room. Mother's Meeting on Mondays in winter months. Seven thirty p.m. and nine p.m. Clothing Club and Provident Club at Church Room on Saturdays at two thirty p.m. Missionary sewing class: Alternate Mondays in Church Room. Guild

Choir: Fourth Monday in month at eight p.m. Worcester Road. Men's Fellowship: every Sunday three forty five p.m. Church Room. Singing class: Tuesdays at Worcester Road. At eight p.m.

St Luke's, Headless Cross. Rector: L. W. Compton M.A. Church-wardens: Mr M. W. Palmer and Mr B. Perkins. Organist: Mr C. G. Lee. Daily evensong at eight p.m. except fridays, that is seven thirty. St Luke's Sunday School: Ten fifteen a.m. and two fifty p.m. Communicants Guild. Women, eight p.m. on Wednesdays preceding First Sunday in month. Lads: Eight fifteen on Thursdays before the first Sunday in the month.

Roman Catholic Church, Mount Carmel, Beoley Road. Built in eighteen thirty two. Cruciform in shape with front tower. Sitting accommodation for three hundred. Priest-in-charge: Rev. Father J. Clement Fowler O.S.B. Organist: Mr B. P. Wells. Licensed for the solemnization of marriages.

Wesleyan Methodist: Circuit Officers: Stewards: Mr T. Grey J.P. "Netherstead", Studley. Mr C. Wright, Fifty Four, Bromsgrove Road. Sec: Mr R. W. Denny, one hundred and ninety six, Mount Pleasant. Sec: Local Preacher's Meeting: Mr T. Hewitt, Rectory Road. Circuit Sunday School Council: Sec: Mr Howard Bird, Rectory Road.

Bates Hill Chapel: Minister: Rev. B. Crosby. Society Stewards: Mr A. E. Crow and Mr W. Terry. Poor Stewards: Mr T. H. Hughes and Mr A. G. Silk. Chapel Stewards: Mr W. Simmonds and Mr W. Houghton. Treasurer: Mr A. Simmonds. Sec: Mr T. Hewitt. Choirmaster: Mr F. J. Whiteley. Organist: Mr F. Laugher. Licensed for the solemnization of Marriages. Guild: Tuesdays, seven forty five. Treasurer: Mrs. W. H. Jarvis. Sec: Miss N. Johnson. Sixty seven, Oakley Road. Band of Hope: Saturday Superintendent: Mr F. J. Whiteley. Dorcas Society: Sec: Mrs J. W. Shrimpton and Miss Shrimpton. Ladies Association: Sec: Miss Munslow. Treasurer: Mrs. A. Farr. Holyoake's Field Mission: Sundays at six thirty p.m. Treasurer: Mr C. Terry. Sec: Mr E. Clarke, one hundred and two, Easemore Road. Holyoake's Field Sunday School: Sup: Mr A. E. Edkins. Holyoake's Field Band of Hope: Sec: Mr J. Mobberley.

Holyoake's Field Brotherhood: Sunday afternoons. Pres: Mr H. Higgs. Headless Cross Chapel: Rev. J. A. Asquith Baker "Epworth", Rectory Road. Society Stewards: Mr T. Ward and Mr A. V. Terry. Poor Stewards: Mr C. Chinn and Mr A. Haden. Organist and Choirmaster: Mr W. H. Fountain.

Sunday Schools: Sup: G. H. Rollins and Mr J. Moore. Sec: Mr W. M. Haden. Dorcas Society: Sec: Mrs Farr. Treasurer: Mrs J. H. Harper.

Bible Class: Meetings at Wesleyan Chapel. Sundays at two thirty p.m. Band of Hope: Saturdays at six thirty p.m. Sup: Mr H. Wilkes. Sec: Mr A. Haden. Guild: Meetings on Mondays at eight p.m. Pres: Rev. J. A. Baker. Sec: Mr C. H. Wall.

Congregational: Church at Evesham Street. Sundays at eleven a.m. and six thirty p.m. Minister: Rev. Edgar Todd, "Ardenholme", Beoley Road. Treasurer: Mr P. Spencer. Sec: Mr F. G. Heaphy. Organist: Mr A. Ledbury. Hon. Curator: Mr T. Penn. Resident Trustees: Mr W. E. Hemming and Mr P. Spencer. Caretaker: Mr A. Cox, Littleworth Cottage. Licensed for the solmnization of marriage.

Baptist: Chapel: Ipsley Green. Minister: Rev. H. E. R. Wassell, Other Road. Sec: Mr A. E. Kettle. Organist: Mr R. F. Dolphin, Bromsgrove Road. Building Fund: Treasurer: Mr T. C. Patchett. Sec: Mr H. W. Perry. Licensed for solemnization of marriage.

Primitive Methodist: Alcester Street Chapel Minister: Rev. J. L. Pritchard, "Wearside', Easemore Road. Society Stewards: Mr T. Wyers and Mr O. E. Eades. Licensed for marriages.

United Methodist: Church at Mount Pleasant. Minister: Rev. W. A. Cooper. Society Stewards: Mr V. H. Mole and Mr G. Douglas. Sec: Mr J. J. Taylor, Mount Pleasant. Circuit Steward: Mr A. M. Cooke. Organist: Mr W. E. Mead. Trust Steward: Mr F. J. Doble. Trust Secretary: Mr V. H. Mole, West Avenue. Licensed for solemnization of marriages.

Christadelphian Meetings: Co-op Hall, George Street. Christians who refuse to be designated. Exposition of Scriptures: Sunday at six thirty. Meeting Place: Walford Street. Sunday "Breaking of Bread" at eleven a.m.

Salvation Army: Barracks at Ipsley Street. Sunday at eleven a.m. and six thirty p.m. Sunday School: ten a.m. and three p.m.

Brotherhoods: Temperance Hall: Sundays at three p.m. until four p.m. Pres: Mr W. C. Freeman. Sec: Mr J. B. Guest, Park Road. Treasurer: Mr A. E. Humphries.

Headless Cross Adult School: Every Sunday at eight a.m. Women. Wednesday nights at Primitive Methodist Chapel.

Register of Licences Granted in the Division of Redditch September 8th 1876

Name of Property	Name and Address of Owner	Name of Licence Holder
Red Lion Inn, Alvechurch	Esther Holliday: Alve	Henderson, John Arch
Swan Inn, Alvechurch	Spencer, Rev. E. Tavistock	Newbould, Hannah
Hopwood Wharf Inn	Parkes, Richard Hopwood	Pettifer, William
Bowling Green Inn, Beoley	Mole, Robert EsQ	Reader, James
Village Inn, Beoley	Spencer, Rev. E. Tavistock	Whitmore, John
Lygon Arms, Feckenham	Bellwing, Elizabeth	Bellwing, George
Rose and Crown do.	James Charles	James, Martha
Red Lion Inn, Hunt End	Spencer, Rev. E. Tavistock	Chambers, Joseph
Red Lion Inn, Astwood Bank	Hollington, George A. B.	Goodyear, William
White Lion Inn. do.	Hemming, Henry	Davis, Charles
Neville Arms, Ridgeway	Ewel, Abergavenny	Green, Rowland
Rose and Crown, Webheath	Spencer, Rev. E. Tavistock	Andrews, William
Fox and Goose, Foxlydiate	Hemming, Richard Bentley	Manor, Shinton John
Lamb and Flag, Unicorn Hill	Davis, Richard	Dunn, Edith
Plough and Harrow, Redditch	Trustees of Whatcoat	Edwards, William
Bell Inn, Britten St.	Sarsons, Mrs Tardibegge	Francis, Edwin
Queen's Head, Br'grove Rd	Spencer, Rev. E. Tavistock	Field, Richard
Crown Inn, Prospect Hill	Freer Leacroft Kingswinford	Hollyoak, William
Fleece Inn, Evesham St.	Wyers, Richard	Pinfield, John
Fox and Goose, Church Green South	Latchfield, Ben	Rowntree, Hugh (Royal)
Sportsman's Arms, Redditch	Spencer, Rev. E. Tavistock	Rickards, Thomas
Golden Cross Inn (Rail?)	Roberts, Frederick	Samuel, Herbert
Unicorn Hotel, Redditch	Spencer, Rev. E. Tavistock	Stinton, Alfred
Vine Hotel (Talbot). do.	Bartleet, Mrs T. M.	Smith, Asan
Red Lion Inn. do.	Smith, Herbert	Webb, James
Fountain Inn. do.	Whele, Emma	Whele, Jessie
Greyhound Inn. do.	Spencer, Rev. E. Tavistock	Croxall, Robert
Holly Bush, Beoley	Ganderton, William	Jeffries, Walter
Yew Tree Inn, Feckenham	English, John	Baker, William
Elcocks Brook, Ham Green	Hopcroft, Ben	Hopcroft, Ben
Fleece Inn, Crabbs Cross	Chambers, Fred	Chambers, Fred
Crown Inn, Crabbs Cross	Morris, Thomas & James	Carwardine, Richard
Seven Stars, Headless Cross	Duggins, John, H. X.	Ralph, Joseph

Name of Property	Name and Address of Owner	Name of Licence Holder
Dog and Pheasant, do.	Townsend Alfred, Finstall	Clarke, Felix
Gate Hangs Well. do.	Mason's Orphanage, B'ham	Emms, Charles
Scale and Compass. do.	Spencer, Rev. E. Tavistock	Johnson, Walter
Red Lion, Inkberrow	Anderson, James	Anderson, James
Stockwood, Inkberrow	Savage, Thomas	Savage, Thomas
Bristol Inn (Rocklands)	Thomas, James	Mobland, George
Woodine Cottage H. X.	Thomas, Sam	Leyston, Mary
White Lion Inn, Red Lion Street	Andrews, Thomas	Andrews, Thomas
Scorpion Inn, Red Lion Street		
Hart Inn, George St.	Gibbs, Mrs Park Road	Beard, John
Oddfellows Arms, Windsor St.	Thomas, James. Clive Rd	Barker, William
Printers Arms, Evesham St.	Cranmore, Moses	Crow, Thomas Upton
Bird-in-the-Hand, George St.	Clarke, Ben	
Woodland Cottage, Mt Pleasant	Trustees Lord Windsor	Cooke, Susannah
Brewers Arms, Windsor St.	Izod, Henry	Crow, William
White Swan, Vine Street (Worc Rd)	White, Elizabeth. Foxlydiate	Duggins, Ann
Cricketers Arms, Beoley Road	Webb, James	Fourt, Thomas
Beehive Inn, Alcester St.	Free, Edmund	Free, Edmund
Railway Tavern, Hewel Rd.	Harvonson Richard. The Cedars	Hollington, W
Kings Arms, Beoley Rd.	Field, John. Alvechurch	Hollington, J
Old Britton, Evesham St.	Whitehouse, George. B'ham	Houghton, David
The Alma Tavern, Ipsley St.	Skinner, Joseph	Hodgetts, William
Brittania Inn, Walford St.	Field, Charles. Littleworth	Huntley, Peter
Golden Salmon, Evesham Street	Webb, William	Mills, Reuben
Shakespeare Tavern	Ben, Brown	Millward, Samuel
The Lamp Tavern, Walford St.	Mills, Mrs Alcester St.	Rickards, George
Rifleman Inn, Park Rd.	Brooks, Isaac	Rudge, James
Royal George, Evesham St.	Gibbs, William	Steward, John
Horse and Jockey. do.	Walford, Thomas. B'ham	Smith, Helen
Nags Head, Alcester St.	Bennett, William. Alcester	St. Wardle, Jane
Bird-in-the-Hand, Walford St.	Ballard, Catherine	Wright, John

Plumbers Arms, Walford St., Volenteers Arms, George St., Scourers Arms, Prospect Hill, The Rising Sun, Alcester St, The Queen's Head, Queen Street, The Golden Lion, Red Lion Street, The Warwick Arms, Ipsley Street, The Foresters Arms, Headless Cross, The Cricketers Arms, Headless Cross, The Jubilee Inn, Edward Street, The Fox Inn, Edward Street, The Unicorn, Top Unicorn Hill, The Black Horse, Mount Pleasant, The Eagle, Crabbs Cross, The Waggon and Horses, Beoley Road, The Fleece Hotel, Crabbs Cross.

Price List Given in Woman's World Book: 1900

"They talk about a woman's sphere, as though it had a limit; There's not a place in earth or heaven, There's not a task to mankind given, There's not a blessing or a woe, There's not a whisper — yea or no, There's not a life, or death or birth, that has a feather-weight of worth, Without a woman in it".

How the sovereign is expended: How we live on 20/-s a week.

Rent	2s-6d
3 cwts coal at 6d per cwt/.	1s-6d
2 qts lamp oil	4d
Candles	1d
Sunlight Soap	5d
1¼ pecks flour at 1/8d per peck	2s-1d
¼ lb yeast	2½d
For baking 5 loaves and a cake	2½d
3 lbs crystal sugar at 1¾d	5¼d
½ lb tea 1/-s	6d
Coffee and cocoa	6d
Vegetables of all sorts	1-6d
Bloaters and kippers	6d
2 lbs bacon at 6d per lb	1-0d
½ lb butter at 1/2d per lb	7d
½ lb margarine at 8d	4d
¾ lb cheese at 6d per lb	4½d
½ lb rice	1d
2 lbs oatmeal	6d
1 lb sultanas	4d
½ lb suet	4d
3 lbs of beef (Sun: Mon: Tues) 1-6d	
Meat and fish during week	1-0d
Weekly investment in Sunday School Clothing Club	6d
Total	17-3¾d

Husband's expenses = Sick Club = 6d Paper and periodicals 6d
Total with main expenses = 18s-3¾d
Surplus left for sundries = 1s-8¼d. Grand Total = £1-0s-0d.

Redditch Organisations

Redditch Angling

Club. Pres: Mr T. Baylis. Sec: Mr R. W. Fisher, "Cinderford" 90, Easemore Road. Club Waters: Binton, Luddington, Salford, Cleeve, Abbots Salford Standard Works Fishing Club (S. Allcock & Co, Ltd). Sec: Mr W. H. Gregory. Abbey Mills Fishing Club. Sec: Mr A. C. Williams.

Redditch Cricket and Hockey Club. Red Lane. Sec. and Treasurer: Mr A. O'Neal 37, Glover Street.

Cricket Section: Sec: Mr A. Moreton, 168, Mount Pleasant.

Hockey Section: Sec: F. W. Rendle, Easemore Road.

Tennis Section: Mr A. Hughes and Mr H. Lowe.

Redditch Golf Round: The Soudan, Cemetery Lane. Pres: Viscount Windsor. Sec: Mr T. C. Patchett. Captain and Treasurer: Mr W. G. Thomas.

Terry's Cricket Club: Cemetery Lane ground. Sec: Mr A. E. Johnson, 34, Evesham Road, Headless Cross.

Redditch and District Motor Cycle Club: Pres: Dr Protheroe Smith. Sec: Mr H. Davis. Headquarters: Unicorn Hotel.

Redditch Football, Bromsgrove Road Ground. Club House, Railway Hotel. Pres: Mr G. W. Hobson. Sec: Mr A. Ledbury, 24, Orchard Street.

Redditch Road and Path Club: Headquarters: Railway Hotel. Pres: Mr W. Smith. Captain: Mr A. L. Pitts. Sec: Mr A. Sealey, Evesham Road.

Redditch and Studley Football: Sec: Mr F. Smith, Rectory Road.

Redditch Swimming Club Baths, Hewel Road.

Pres: Mr R. W. Smith. Hon. Sec: Mr W. A. C. Moule, 28, Evesham Street, Redditch. Clubs: Union Club Ltd, Easemore Road. Chairman Mr E. T. Moule.

Redditch Liberal Club Ltd: Alcester Street.

Treasurer Mr W. W. Baylis, Oakley Road. Sec: Mr W. Hill, "Mostyn" Easemore Road. Steward: J. W. Moore.

Redditch Social Club Ltd: Hodges Memorial Hall. Chairman: Mr G. E. Leach.

Seymour Club: Ipsley Street. Sec: Mr C. H. Edmonds.

St Stephen's Men's Club: Easemore Road. Sec. and Treasurer: Mr C. E. Spooner, Easemore Road, Redditch. St Stephen's Men's Club: Sick and

Dividend Society, Club House, Easemore Road. Sec. and Treasurer: Mr J. F. Shakespeare, George Street.

Church Road Club Ltd: Managing Director: Mr J. F. Smith.

Buffalo Lodges: Friendship Lodge: Market Place. Sec: Mr H. Taylor, Oakly Road. Ferguson Lodge: Warwick Arms Hotel, Ipsley Street. Sec: Mr V. Treadgold, Peakman Street.

Halls: Temperance Hall: Worcester Road. Seats 500. Hallkeeper: Mr J. Forrest.

Plymouth Hall: Easemore Road. Steward: Mr P. Horen.

Masonic Hall: Ipsley Street. W. M. Sec: Mr C. H. Edmunds, Mount Pleasant.

Picture Houses

Bosco's Pictures Ltd: Public Hall: Manager: Mr Ritson.

Picture House, Alcester Street, Proprietress: Mrs Treadgold.

The Redditch Palace Ltd: Alcester Street. Manager: Mr J. Baron.

Other Societies and Organisations: Redditch Temperance Society: Est. 1862. Treasurer: Mr T. H. Hill, 6, Victoria Street.

Taylor And Mills (Redditch) Mutual Self Held Money Society (especially authorised) Sec: Mr R. Williams and Company. Accountants. Reg. office: 268, High Street, Stirchley.

National Union Of Women's Suffrage Societies. Redditch Branch. Hon. Sec: Miss Alice Milward. Foxlydiate House. Treasurer: Mr H. A. Pearson.

Redditch Billposting Company: 4.a, Bromsgrove Road and 49, Unicorn Hill.

Manufacturers' Protection Society. Redditch Plate Glass Association. Treasurer: Mr S. L. Huins. Sec. and Agent: Mr J. P. Morris. Evesham Street.

Hospital Saturday Fund. Chairman: Mr J. Warner. Hon. Sec: Mr. W. Hill.

Nursing Association. Pres: Rev: Canon Newton. Sup: Mr R. W. Smith and Miss Isobel Smith. Sec: Mr S. G. Beacham, Ipsley Mount. Redditch.

Redditch Amateur Society: Hon. Treasurer: Mr G. Galbraith. Sec: Mr P. T. Evans, "Rossleigh", Park Road.

Male Voice Choir and Madrigal Society: meets Thursdays at Baptist Church, Ipsley Street. Conductor: Mr A. Hodges. Sec: Mr A. Crow, St George's Road.

Redditch and District Flying Club: Plough and Harrow, Evesham Street. Sec: Mr T. J. Boswell, 202, Mount Pleasant.

Redditch and District License Holders Association. Royal Hotel. Sec: Mr A. Smith.

Operative Society of Bricklayers. Vine Inn, Evesham Street. Sec: Mr A. Melley, Birchfield Road.

Amalgamated Society of Carpenters and Joiners: Vine Inn. Sec: Mr W. Bevan, Lodge Road.

Amalgamated Society of House Decorators and Painters: Vine Inn. Sec: Mr R. H. Hall, High Street, Studley.

Redditch Master Builders Association. Pres: Mr A. E. Edkins. Sec: Mr Fred Turner, Ivor Road.

Amalgamated Society of Gas Workers and General Labourers: Sec: Mr E. Peak, Clive Road.

Redditch Fire Brigade: Captain: W. Jameson.

Redditch District and Fire Brigades' Association. Sec: Mr G. G. Sharp, 28, Mount Street.

Bands: Redditch Town Band: Bandmaster: Mr P. Spencer, Junior, Ipsley Street.

"A" Company 3rd Battalion. Worcestershire Regiment. Band-master: Mr A. L. Harris.

Imperial Band: Band-master: Mr T. N. Bates.

Spencer's Band: Band-master: Mr C. Spencer, Music Warehouse, Evesham Street.

Redditch Brotherhood Band: Band-master: Mr. W. Dean.

Wilkes's String Band: Band-master: Mr. E. Wilkes.

Newspapers: Redditch Indicator (ld) Published Friday Evenings.

Boy Scouts: Pres: Right Hon: Earl of Plymouth. Chairman: Mr L. F. Lambert. Commissioner: Mr W. H. Wiggin.

Troops: 1st Redditch, 2nd Redditch, Studley, Alvechurch, Whythall, Hewell, Headless Cross, Hon. Sec: Mr Arthur T. Hughes, "Oakleigh", Easemore Road.

Scoutmasters: 1st Redditch: Mr R. G. Spencer 78, Other Road. 2nd. Redditch: Mr C. T. White, 45, Evesham Street. Studley: Mr R. H. Feasey, Station Road, Studley. Alvechurch: Mr W. H. Wiggan. Bordesley Hall: Miss Wiggin, Bordesley Hall. Wythall: Captain Johnstone. Hewell: Mr L. F. Lambert (pro-tem). Headless Cross: Mr C. T. White (pro-tem).

The old Fire Station was at the top of Park Road. The engine being drawn by two horses and the Captain was Mr Harry Bough. The old Council offices were at Park Road and Front Hill, Mr Jameson being in charge. I understand from reports that Plymouth Road was built by the council workers themselves and cut through the Old Soudan about 1914, and, about 1930 there was a terrific cloudburst which completely flooded the lower half of Plymouth Road and the whole of the Railway Station.

The old Pawn-Shop in George Street was run by the Skinner family, but the main Wardrobe Dealer was Granny Ross, Unicorn Hill. Full title and the Address: Mrs M. A. Ross. Wardrobe Dealer, 39, Unicorn Hill, Redditch.

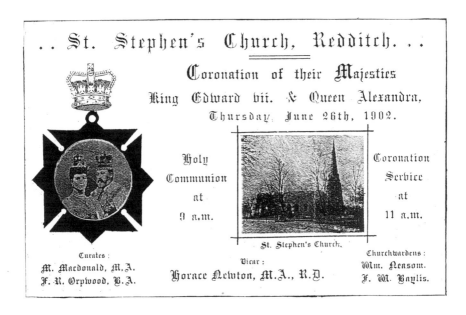

Business People In Redditch In 1936

Allen, Frank and Son. Electrical Contractors.
Atkins Arthur. Cardboard Box Manufacturers.
Bate, W. G. Plumber, etc.
Beacham and Gregory Co Ltd.
Beacon Insurance Co Ltd.
Bright, H. A. Builder.
Brown, W. and W. Coal Merchants.
Brough, G. F. Tailor.
Chronical Printing Office.
Cranmore, Simmonds and Co Ltd. (Ironmongers).
Darvill and Baker. Mineral Water Manufacturers.
Davis. A. E. Tobacconist and Newsagent.
Dixon, T. and M. Coal Merchants.
Edkins and Sons, Grocers and Newsagents.
Ellis, T. P. Cakes, Cooked Meats.
Fosters. Studley (Ironmongers).
Goodall and Company. Cardboard Box Manufacturers.
Harbon, G. H. Music Warehouse. Church Green East.
Harris, C. Radio Stores.
Hadley, E. Estate Agent.
Harrison, W. and Company. Opticians.
Heaphy, F. G.
Hallam, G. and Company. Sheffield.
Helical Casting Reel Company.
Hemming Thom. F. Estate Agent.
Hodges. E. A. Stationers.
Hopkins, G. F. and Son. Opticians.
Horton, G. H. and Son. Motor Garage.
Huins James. Boots and Shoes.
Huntley, B. J. Funeral Furnishers.
Hughes, A. Tobacconist.
Jones Harold Ltd. Coal Merchants.
Layton Electric Co Ltd.
Ludford's Family Hotel.
Martin and Pethard. Insurance Brokers.
Millward, J. and A. Painters and Decorators.
Midland Red Bus Company.

Mitchell, J. and W. Paper Mkrs.
Mills Bros. Builders.
Morris (Redditch). Ltd. Drapers.
Neasom and White. Auctioneers.
Palmers Corn Stores.
Parr, H. and Sons Ltd. Paper Merchants.
Pitts. (Redditch) Ltd. Motor Garage. Evesham Street.
Redditch Indicator. Easemore Road.
Redditch Steam Laundry. Bromsgrove Road.
Redditch Building Supplies Ltd.
Rose. F. W. and Son. Shoeing Smith.
Rudge, A. E. and Son. Angling Specialists.
Sages. Drapers. 2 and 4, Bates Hill.
Sheldon, R. G. 11, Alcester Street. Newsagent.
Sally. Milliner.
Shrimpton and Mobberley. Coal Merchants.
Smith and Spencer. Mineral Water Manufacturers.
S. W. S. Electric Power Co Ltd. Showrooms. Evesham Street.
Studley Garage and Engineering Works.
Tarleton, H. B. Builder.
Thomas, L. and M. T. Fancy Repository. 19, Evesham Street.
Thompson, B. R. Butcher. 51, Alcester Street.
Tongue, E. A. Undertaker. 22, Park Road.
Townend Walter. Marine Stores.
Townsend, H. T. Brewer.
Turner, A. J. Coal Merchant.
Webbs. Bakers and Seed Merchants. Church Green East.
Wheatley, J. and Sons. Printers.
Wilkes, H. Newsagents. Railway Approach.
Willetts Bros. Butchers. 16, Evesham Street.
Williams, F. Watchmaker. 192, Mount Pleasant.
Wright John and Son. Timber Merchants. Redditch and Studley.
Wyatt, E. W. Monumental Sculptor. Plymouth Road.

List Of Adopted Streets In Redditch Urban District. December, 1935

Arthur Street. Ash Tree Road. Astwood Lane. Adelaide Street. Albert Street (Astwood Bank). Alcester Street. Archer Road. Avenue Road (Astwood Bank). Astwood Road (Feckenham). Alcester Road (Feckenham). Beaufort Street. Birchfield Road. Bromsgrove Road. Britten Street. Bridge Street. Bromfield Road. Birmingham Road.

Birmingham Road (Bordesley). Beoley Road. Bates Hill. Birchensdale Road. Bridley Moor Road. Brockhill Lane. Butler Street (Astwood). Charles Street. Church Green East. Church Green West. Clive Road. Crabbs Cross Lane. Crumpfields Lane. Church Road (Astwood). Church Road (Webheath). Church Road (Redditch). Castle Street (Astwood). Dark Lane (Astwood). Evesham Street. Evesham Road (Headless Cross). Evesham Road (Crabbs Cross). Evesham Road (Astwood Bank). Edward Street. Easemore Road. Enfield Road (Hunt End). Elm Road. Feckenham Road (Headless Cross). Feckenham Road (Astwood Bank). Feckenham Road (Hunt End). Farm Road. Featherbed Lane (Hunt End). Foregate Street (Astwood Bank). Glover Street. Grove Street. George Street. Grange Road. Hazel Road. Hill Street (Unicorn Hill). Hewell Road. Holloway Lane. Heathfield Road (Webheath). High Street (Astwood Bank). High Street (Feckenham). Ivor Road. Ipsley Street. Ipsley Row. Lodge Road. Ludlow Road. Market Place. Mason Road. Marsen Road. Millsborough Road. Mount Street. Mount Pleasant. Melen Street. Mill Lane. New Street. Oakley Road. Orchard Street. Oswald Street. Other Road. Parson's Road. Park Road. Peakman Street. Plymouth Road. Prospect Hill. Prospect Road. Pumphouse Lane (Webheath). Queen Street. Queen Street (Astwood Bank). Red Lion Street. Rectory Road. Retreat Street (Astwood Bank). Salop Road. Salter's Lane. Sillins Avenue. Smallwood Row. Smallwood Street. Smith Street. South Street. Summer Street. St George's Road. Stevenson Avenue. Studley Road. The Square (Feckenham). Tipping's Hill (Hunt End). Unicorn Hill. Victoria Street. Walford Street. West Street. Wellington Street. William Street. Windsor Street. Worcester Road. Walkwood Road (Hunt End).

List Of Unadopted Streets And Roads In The Urban District. December 1935

Arrow Road. Chapel Street (Headless Cross). Gorton's Arch. Highfield Road (Headless Cross). Jubilee Avenue (Headless Cross). Littleworth (off Evesham Street). Malvern Road. Marlpit Lane (Feckenham Road). Mayfields (Mount Pleasant). New Road (Astwood Bank). Rookery Road (Headless Cross). Southmead Avenue (Millsborough Road). West Avenue (off South Street). Woodside Avenue (off Birchfield Road). Yvonne Road (Headless Cross).

The Geographical County of Warwick comprises an area of 629,024 acres. It is divided into four hundreds, and 15 Petty Sessional Divisions, and has two County Boroughs, viz, the Cities of Birmingham and

Coventry, and 240 Civil Parishes. The Administrative County contains 1,798 miles of County Roads. Population of Administrative County for middle of 1934 was 366,550.

Area of the Urban District on December 31st 1932 was 6,076 acres. Area of the Urban District from 1933 was 12,002 acres.

Reduced rateable value, 31st December 1935 – – – – – –

Redditch £71,472.   Feckenham Urban £12,038.
Upper Ipsley £17,886.   Ipsley £5,634.
                                      Feckenham £8,927.
                                      = £115,957.

Population of the Parish in
        1861:   5,541.
do   do   1871:   6,737.
"   "   1881:   7,587.
"   "   1891:   8,227.
Urban District
Council in   1891:   11,311.
"   "   1901:   13,493.
"   "   1911:   15,463.
"   "   1921:   16,235.
"   "   1931:   19,280.
"   "   from 1933.   22,250.
"   "   1989:   78,023.
              1.6.92:   79,623.

Local Governing Bodies: Urban District Council: 1936:

The Urban District Council meet at 6.45 p.m. on the first Monday in the month, at the Council House, Evesham Street. Chairman, George Edward Whitmore, J. P. 56, Rectory Road. Headless Cross, Redditch. Vice-Chairman: Charles Wright, 54, Bromsgrove Road, Redditch.

Members:

No. 1. North Central Ward: James Blackford, Ernest Henry Dyer, Jesse Guise.

No. 2. South Central Ward: Arthur L. Davies, George E. Whitmore, Charles Wright.

No. 3. North West Ward: Charles Henry Blackford, John W. Hughes, George White.

No. 4. North East Ward: Thos. Wm. Hollis, John E. Wilkinson, Arthur Pinfield Wells.
No. 5. Crabbs Cross Ward: John W. Bird, Alfred Wm. Mogg, James Henry Taylor.
No. 7 Feckenham Ward: Frank Bradley, John Havilah Yeomans, Fred Hill.

Officials:
Clerk and Solicitor: M. W. Coupe. Treasurer and Accountant: J. Wright. Council House Rating and Valuation Officer and Registrar of Local Housing Bonds: J. Wright. Medical Officer: Dr. A. B. Follows. Surveyor: L. O. Wilkes. Sanitary and Meat Inspector: W. Jameson. Libraria: A. D. Lewis. Representative on the Old Age Pensions Committee: Jesse Guise.

General Rates:
Rating and Valuation Officer: J. Wright. Collector of Taxes: T. Lomas. Hours: 9 a.m. to 1 p.m. then 2.30 to 5 p.m. Saturdays: 9 a.m. to 12.30 p.m. Attendances at Manor House, Astwood Bank. Fridays only, 2 p.m. to 4.30 p.m.

Redditch Police Division:
Divisional Police Station: Church Road, Redditch. Telephone No. 19. Superintendent: Thomas W. Arey. Inspector: Frank S. Henning. Sub Police Stations: Astwood Bank: Sergeant W. Adams. Telephone No. 8. Wythall: Sergeant F. R. Bache. Telephone No. 10. Constables Out-Stations: Alvechurch. Astwood Bank, (Dark Lane), Beoley, Feckenham, Headless Cross, Hollywood, (Wythall), Inkberrow, Ipsley, and Webheath. (All on telephone).

Redditch Petty Sessions:
Held at the Police Station, Redditch every Wednesday, at 10.30 a.m. and any other day when necessary except Statutory Bank Holidays. Magistrates: Lieut. Col. C. F. Milward. (Chairman) D. McMichael. Col. W. H. Wiggin. H. T. Milward. H. M. Hill. C. Terry. T. E. Cash. B. Woodridge. Miss M. T. Newton. G. E. Whitmore. Major F. Smith. and Wythall Justices. Clerk: T. B. Pritchett, Barclays Bank Chambers, Market Place, Redditch.

County Court:
The Redditch District includes Alvechurch, Astwood Bank, Beoley, Bentley (Upper), Bentley (Lower), Barnt Green, Cofton Hackett, Tutnal

and Cobley, Crabbs Cross, Cross Lanes, Feckenham, Foxyldiate, Headless Cross, Hunt End, Ipsley, Kendal End, Oldberrow, Redditch and Rowney Green. Judge: His Honour Judge Kennedy, K. C. Registrar and High Bailiff: W. H. Scott. Treasurer: The Treasury, Whitehall. Under Bailiff: J. Broom. Hours of Attendance at Registrar's Office from 10 to 4. except Saturdays, when the Office is open from 9 till 12. Offices: Prospect Hill.

Income Tax Officials:
Clerk to the Commissioners sitting at Droitwich, W. .H. Scott, Bromsgrove. Collector for Redditch, Alvechurch, Barnt Green, Beoley, Tardebigge, Bentley Pauncefoot, Tutnall and Cobley. Chief Collector: Birmingham West Area, Lancaster House, 67, Newhall Street, Birmingham.
Collector for Upper Ipsley: J. H. Bomford, Alcester.
Collector for Feckenham and Feckenham Urban: E. Dyer. Church Green.
Inspectors: Weights and Measures: A. Greening, 52, Woodfield Road, King's Heath, Birmingham.
Inspector of Factories and Workshops: A. G. Lotinga, 174, Corporation Street, Birmingham.

Redditch (including Webheath) Directory 1936:

Adelaide Street: 1. Freeman, L. 3. Woodbridge, W. 5. Field, Miss. 7. Styler, Mrs. 9. Louch Jesse. 11. Lewis Clarence. 13. Houghton, W. 15. Taylor, W. 15a. Willis, A. 17. Ashford, Mrs A. 19. Higgins, H. back Bourne, A. 21. Bourne, H. 23. Bourne, A. 27. Parker, W. 29. Beard, Mrs.

Albert Street: 1. Thomas, E. 2. Govier, Mrs. 3. Hall, Mrs. 4. Hartley, A. 5. Haycock, B. 7. James, C. 8. Birch, A. 9. Truscott, Emily W. 10. Noeland, D. 12. Ladbury, A. 14. Finch, Mrs W. F. 16. Hill, A. 18. Sealey, F. 30. Taylor, A. 32. Watson, R. 34. Sheen, E. 36. Blizzard, D. 38. Taylor, Mrs A. E. 40. Hayden, H. 42. Gregory, W. H. 44. Onions, H. 46. Neiland, Mrs. 48. Harris, L. 50. Garraway, Edwin. 52. Jones, A. 54. Cotton, W. 56. Finch, T. 60. Yoxall, F. 62. Mynott, W. G. 64. Hitchman, Miss. 66. Webb, Mrs. 68. Yates, Mrs. 70. Mogg, Mrs. 72. Powell, W. 74. Perks, R. 85. The Patent Ferrule Company. Poole and Sons. The Dairy. Redditch Pure Milk Company Ltd. R. A. Goodall and Company, Peak Works (W. Guest Proprietor).

Alcester Street: 1. Murdoch, Jas. 3. Dyer, J. and Son. 3a. Palmer, T. 3b. Francis, Mrs B. 5. Sally. 6. Meylan, J. L. 7. Field, Mrs. 9. Crook, B. 9a. Street, S. P. 11. Sheldon, R. G. 13. Pearman, H. R. 15. Barrett, R and D. 17. Jones, J. W. 19. Palmer's Corn Stores. 21. Hedges Chemist Ltd. 23. Mole Florence G. 23a. Blundell, L. V. Nag's Head Inn (Reuben Street. Proprietor). 24. Harris George. 26. Coulson, Mrs. 27. Jarvis, A. C. 28. Galbraith, J. 29. The Rising Sun (Edgington, J. W. Proprietor). 30. Millward, J. and A. 31. Steele Bros. 32. Avery, Harry. 33. Dyer, J. and Son. 34. Cash Meat Stores. back 34. Young, F. 35. Shakles, A. G. 36. Fowkes, J. H. 37. Canham, H. 38. Tayler, T. H. 39. Williams' Cafe. 40. Ladbury and Sons. 41. Formston and Son. 41a. and 43. Hewston, J. A. The Palace Theatre. Redditch Liberal Club (Steward W. Merry). 42. Lane, L. back 42. Townsend, W. 44. Langston, Miss. back 44. Brewster Misses M. and L. 46. Ideal Benefit Society. 47. Newman, H. W. (Greengrocer). 48. Johnson, G. F. 49. Baylis, E. 50. Graver, S. 51. Thompson, B. R. 52 to 54. Days, F. T. 53. Lawrence, A. H. 53a. Hill Hemming. 55. Harbon, W. E. Pool Place Garage. The Select Cinema. The Ladies' Realm. Vincent, D. Walton, H. Huins, C. G. and Sons. Pool Place.

Archer Road: Church Institute. 2. Sealey, H. 4. Cooper, Mrs Marsden. (R. S. P. C. A. Inspector). 5. Webster, W. H. 6. Hill, Miss Alcie. 7. Stanton, J. 8. Wyers, Mrs. 9. Green, W. 11. Smith, George. 13. Paddock William. 15. Humphries, H. W. 18. Wright, A. 19. Brown, J. F. 20. Jarvis, Mrs W. 21. Wilkinson, C. A. 22. Wilson, E. T. 23. Bunn, L. O. 24. Dollis, W. 25. King, H. 26. Locke, F. 27. Tay, Miss. 28. Wedgbury, H. 29. Adams, Thomas. 30. Bott, Mrs. 31. Portman, S. 32. Clarke, A. 33. Blundell, T. 34. Harris, V. T. 35. Laight, W. H. 36. Layton, R. 37. Treadgold, R. 38. Smith, Albert. 39. Tay, C. 40. Allbutt, G. F. 41. Duggins, V. N. 43. Wilkinson, S. 45. Benton, H. 47. Crow's Stores. 49. Jones, Emma. 51. Baker, W. 52. Reynolds, C. H. 55. Johnson, S. 57. Mutton, J. 59. Crumpton, G. H. 61. Sealey, Florence. 63. Bullock, T. 65. Sealey, Charles. 67. Floyd William. 69. Thomas, F. 71. Hurst, J. and Son. 73. Turner, Samuel. 75. Penny, George. 77. Hollis, G. H. 79. Smith, W. 81. Parsons, Mrs D. 83. Smith, Lucy. 85. Bearcroft, F. 87. Hill, Henry. 97. Pritchard, E. W. 99. Crow, O. 101. Cooper, C. T. 103. Crow, W. 105. Kelly, A. 107. Crow, Clarrie.

Arrow Road: 1. Rice, H. J. 2. Moore, C. R. 3. Long, Victor. 4. Galbraith, G. 5. Garner, W. 6. Griffin, Albert. 7. Hands, F. 41. Knighton, H. 43. Wedgbury, H. 45. Dolphin, E. 49. Parker, Oliver. 51. Barker, W. 53. Field, M. J. 55. Harper, R. 57. Hemming, W. H. 59. Forman, F. 63. Gilder, H. 65. Langfield, W. H. 67. Barton, Mrs C. 69. Perkins, S. C. 71. Hack, G. Ryder, H "Fernleigh".

Arthur Street: 1. Merry, F. S. 2. Dawkes, M. 3. Wheeler, F. 4. Nash, A. 5. Andrews, G. 6. Dilling, B. 7. Baylis, E. 8. Keyte, V. J. 9. Mills, W. 10. Clayton, Mrs. 11. Edwards, W. 12. Wilcox, A. A. 13. Keeling, W. E. 14. Dudley, A., 15. Stockley, H. 16. Field, F. 18. Danks, C. 20. Hemming, T. 22. Hopkins, V. 24. Rose, C. 26. Mogg, Gilbert. 28. Dudley, A. F. 30. Chambers, A. 32. Boswell, G. F. 34. Dyer, A. 36. Ramm, Mrs. 38. Stokes, V. 40. Bonham, J. 42. Sealey, E. 44. East, Oliver. 46. Louch, W. 48. Warren, C.

Ash Tree Road: 1. Timms, W. H. 2. Miles, B. N. 3. Stanley, G. F. 4. Sullivan, P. H. 5. Troth, A. 6. Willis, H. 7. Adams, J. 8. Gittuss, A. 9. Keyte, J. 10. Berry, J. E. 19. Harris, J. H. 21. Jenkins, W. H. 23. Wheeler, Silas. 25. Hooper, Kate. 27. Bradley, W. 29. Hill, G. W. 31. Baylis, Lewis. 33. Gaize, G. J. 35. Maries, A. G. 37. Banks, Catherine. 39. Gibbs, H. 41. Heaton, A. H. 43. Stanley, R. 45. Onberry, W. 47. Twinbru, E. 49. Street, E. G. 51. Murray, A. J. 53. Hudson, A. H.

Batchley Road: 1. Ashborne, A. 2. Batson, D. 3. James, C. 4. Stowe, W. 5. Brazil, H. F. 6. Crow, E. J. 7. Dunn, A. 8. Swinborne, A. 9. Locke, H. T. 10. Beard, A. 11. Warren, A. 12. Poole, W. 13. Clarke, F. W. 14. Houghton, H. 15. Betterton, E. 16. Duggins, H. 17. Hopcroft, J. 18. Styler, Mrs A. M. 19. Partridge, H. 20. Wilkes, W. 21. Jones, B. 22. Griffin, H. 23. Blackford, G. 24. Watson, S. 25. Stanley, W. 26. Dyer, J. 27. Griffiths, L. 28. Wingfield, E. 29. Duffin, E. 30. White, A. 31. Brandon, W. 32. Moore, C. 33. Bott, W. H. 34. Ladbury, J. F. 35. Johnson, Mrs. 36. Tustin, W. 37. Shelton, W. F. 38. Smith, W. V. 39. Reynolds, F. 40. Betteridge, Mrs A. 41. Turner, F. G. 42. Giles, V. 43. Baylis, T. 44. Prescott, A. 45. Field, W. H. 47. Clarke, A. 49. Shaw, S. F. 51. Emus, Mrs Emma. 53. Taylor, W. 55. Pemberton, A. 57. Danks, J. 59. Hartigan, J. J. 61. Poole, E. 63. Hurst, P. 65. Harris, H. 67. Hunt, C. 69. Simmons, F. 71. Ramsey, E. 73. King, Miss. 75. Sealey, H. 77. Jobson, E. 81. Lewis, G. E. 83. Crow, A. 85. Ingram, A. E. 87. Lewis, L. 89. Stockley, J. 91. Pinfield-Wells, A. 93. Shaw, H. 95. Spiers, H. 97. Rees, W. J. 99. Styler, F. H. 101. Browning, H. 103. Cull, C. 105. Bunegar, W. H. 107. Blundell, G. 109. Maries, J. 111. Moss, J. A. 113. Wharrad, A. 115. Phillips, A.

Bates Hill: Sage, J. R. Drapers. 6. Price, J. 8. Lazell, A. 10. Chester, H. 12. Palmer, Mrs. 14. Johnson, J. 16. Wedgbury, F. T. 18. Britcher, J. 20. Dobbins, G. F. Wagstaff. Rev. H.O. Mills Frank (Cycles). Lee, F. Lee Lock Works. Dyer, E. H. Old Factory Mills. Lee, M. and Son. Old Factory Mills. Custerton R. Old Factory. Smout, C. Old Factory. Warren James and Company. Old Factory. Hemming, W. Direct Fishing Tackle Company. Old Factory. 22. Bates Hill, Thomas, Miss M. T.

Beaufort Street: 2. Baines, J. and Son. 4. Candy, F. 6. Aspindale, Mrs. 8. Savery, W. 9. Shepard, J. Shepard, Mrs. 10. Malin, E. 12. Gardener, G. 14. Cooke, G. 16. Hollier, H.

Beoley Road: 1. Alcester Co-Operative Company Ltd. 1a. Proudfoot, J. King's Arms Inn. (Lawford Horace, A. Proprietor) 2. Wiggett, H. F. 4. Shaw, A. 6. Bagnal, H. 7. James, L. 8. Randle, Miss. 9. Eaves, R. 10. Thornton, W. 11. Perkins, F. 12. Duggins, J. 13. Huins, M. A. 14. Russell, W. 15. Priddy, Miss. 16. Cave Rev. 17. Lewis, A. 18. James, A. 19. Chisholm, R. 20. Cross, J. Green Sid. 21. Pearce, T. 22. Hill, Miss C. E. 23. Atkins, Arthur. 24. Booker and Company. 25. Baylis, H. 26. Cooke, E. 27. Baylis, John. 28. Webb, Edmund. 29. Grant, F. 30. Field, Mrs. 31. Butler, J. 31a. Bird, S. 32. Hemming, E. E. 33. Allcock, H. W. 34. Gibbs, A. 35. Ellis, H. B. 36. Herbert, H. 37. Ellis, A. 38. Hancox,

H. 39. Smith, E. 40. Howes, Laura. 41. Treadgold, F. 42. Brown, F. 43. Heath, Benjamin. 44. Cottrill, F. J. 45. Twigg, R. 46. Lewis, C. 47. Taylor, P. G. 48. Perry, J. W. 49. Guest, Mrs. 50. Wythes, Miss. 51. Burrow, A. E. 52. Sealey, E. 53. Eades, M. V. 54. Trueman, J.

Beoley Road: 55. Craddock, A. 56. Floyd, William. 57. Buckley, J. 58. Potter, H. 59. Scarrett, A. 60. Tongue, J. 61. Brown, W. 62. Baylis, T. and Company. 64. Layton, H. 65. Kings, Miss. 66. Davis, E. R. 67. Waring, Mrs. 68. Bloom, F. 69. Horton, Mrs. 70. Emms, George. 71. Harbon, Mrs. 71a. Billingsley, A. 72. Cocking, H. 73. Harbon, Mrs. 74. Styler, A. 75. Wilkins, George. 76. Pretty, G. 77. Sealey, Mrs. 78. Wall, L. 79. Smith, P. 80. Preece, M. 81. Croxall, S. 82. Evans, S. 83. Quinney, C. 85. Pinfield, Mrs. 87. Hawkes, J. 89. Webb. S. T. 90. Baylis, Charles. 91. Baylis, William. 93. Court, F. 94. Clarke, Mrs. 95. Green, J. 96. Carwardine, A. 97. Watton, A. 98. Baylis, J. 99. Cooke, J. 100. Smith, Mrs, Symons, Mrs, V. Smith, Misses Neptune House. Smith, W. and Son. Neptune Works. 104. Beckington, A. G. 105. Tongue, E. K. 106. Carr, E. 107 and 109. Hanson John. 107a. McHugh, F. back 107. Carwardine, L. 107b. Anker, E. back McHugh, H. 108. Morris, A. 110. Wall, S. 112. Morton, Miss. 114 and 116. Long, F. Butcher. 118. Laugher, Herman. 120. Hicks, J. 121. Hall, F. H. 122. Sealey, A. 123. Duffin, H. 124. Owen, Mary. 125. Simmons, R. Simmons, F. 126. Garner, Miss. 127. Rigby, R. 128. Duggins, F. T. 129. Farr, W. 130. Duggins, J. 131. Batson, F. 132. Duggins, Misses E. and W. 133. Jones, Mrs. 134. Nash, E. 135. Rider, S. 136. Perks, T. 137. Smart, R. 138. Morris, G. 139. Nibbs, A. 140. Simmons, T. 141. Hill, H. 142. Sparry, H. 143. Yates, E. 144. Clarke, A. 145. Batson, G. 146. Clarke, Mrs. 147. Rider, J. 148. Ball, H. G. 149. Smith, E. 150. Webb, E. 152. Brookes, G. 153. Hunt, E. T. 154. Griffin, H. 155. Tunnycliffe, H. 156. Smith, A. 157. Baylis, R. 158. Lawrence, George. 159. Ames, J. 160. Horton, W. 161. Day, Mrs A. 162. Bradshaw, E. 163. Hill, P. 164. Wheeler, W. 165. Such, H. 166. Morrall, F. 167. Sutton, Miss. 168. Faulkner, A. 169. Harrison, A. 170. Hemming, F. 171. Phillpot, P. 172. Moseley, J. 173. Bromley, Miss C. 174. Clarke, E. 175. Dyson, Misses. 176. Eames, A. J. 177. Bradshaw, J. W. 178. Street, G. F. 179. Warmington, A. 180. Smith, J. 181. McClenn, C. 182. Creed, H. 183. Kings, W. 184. Mills, J. 185. Garner, A. E. 186. Smith, A. E. 187. Yoxall, Mrs. 188. Winfield, E. 189. Bradbury, T. 190. Pinfield, G. 191. Hiscock, H. 192. Pettifer, H. 193. Brewster, W. 194. James, C. 195. Fowkes, H. 196. White, Mrs. 197. Davis, Mrs. 198. Curtis, S. 199. Simons, T. 200. Chatwin, F. 201. Young, H. 202. Bassett, W. 203. Hitchen, G. 204. Griffin, C. 205. Leaver, Mrs. 205a. Preece, H. 207.

Baylis, A. C. 209. Weyham, Mrs. 211. Chiles, A. 213. Ingram, J. 215.
Woodbridge, D. 217. Lewis, Mrs. 219. Young, W. H. 221. Gazey, J.
223. Knight, Mrs. 225. Long, Mrs. 227. Davis, W. 229. Farr, S. A. 231.
Whadcoat, H. 233. Twigg, C. 235. Burgess, W. 237. Spiers, F. 239.
Cross, F. 241. George, A. 243. Day, H. 245. Simmons, B. 247. Curtis, B.
249. Hemming, J. 251. Apperley, Ernest. 253. Gazey, F. W. 255.
Hardman, F. 257. Hopcroft, B. 259. Haden, F. 261. Freeman, Mrs. 263.
Taylor. 265. Hunt, D. 267. Burgen, W. 269. Seymour, T. 271. Hawkes,
L. H. 273. Tracey, F. 275. Sealey, L. 277. Hemming, A. 279. Styler, J.
281. Preece, F. A. 283. Cox, J. W. 285. Davis, H. 287. Preece, S. 289.
Cashmore, F. 291. Simmons, H. 293. Clarke, B. 295. Andrews, W. 297.
Corbett, J. 299. Emery, T. W. 301. Webb, C. 303. Gittins, S. 309.
Cooke, A. 311. Merrill, E. 313. Pinfield-Wells, K. 317. Snellgrove, J.
319. Brazier, F. J. 321. Sanders, J. 323. Walton, C. 325. Lewis, E. 327.
Rice, R. 329. Linwell, W. J. 331. Jones, G.

In 1917 it is recorded that Mr A. E. Edwards kept the Cricketers'
Arms. Beoley Road.

Also Mr R. Edwards kept the Greyhound Inn Prospect Hill.

Beoley Road Cottages: (off Beoley Road). 1. Drew, T. 2. Checketts, G.
3. Foster, E. 4. Bird, J. 5. Baylis, R. 6. Ludworth, R. 7. Strain, A. 8.
Peasgood, D., James, Mr A., Smith, Mrs.

Evesham Street: Huins James. Cranmore, Simmons and Company
Ltd. 3. Hodges, A. E. 5. Boots Ltd. 6. Griffiths, A. L. 7. Preedy and
Sons Ltd. 8. DeGreys Ltd. 9. Taylor's. 10. Jones Bros. 11. British and
Argentine Meat Company. 13. Brough, G. F. 14. Hopkins, G. F. and
Son Ltd. 15. Watkins, H. E. 16. Willets Bros. 18. Melen, F. 19.
Thomas, Miss. 20. Morris John, Grocer. 21. Hopkins, G. F. and Son
Ltd. 22. Johnson Bros. 23. Maypole Dairy Co. Ltd. 24. Harrison, W.
and Company. 25. Rigby Davis (Ladies Clothes). 26. Nicholls, F. G.
27 – 33. Hollington, F. W. and Company. 28. Moule William Ltd
(Chemist). 30. Snelgar Reginald. 32. S. W and S Power Company Ltd.
36. Wilson, J. V. and Company. 34. The London Central Meat
Company. 35. Barclay, F. 37. Halford Cycle Company. 38. Home and
Colonial Tea Stores. 93. Mason George Ltd. (Grocers). 40. Burton
Montague, Ltd. 41. Dewhurst, J. H. Ltd. 42. The Octagon Library. 43.
Smith, Tom (Greengrocer) 44. Peeks. 45. Humphries, Wm and Sons. 46.
Firth's Waterproof Clothing Company. Congregational Church. 47.
Pearks' Stores (Grocer). 48. Kays, ways, pays. 49. Foster Bros. 50. Burn,
Fred. 51. Bate, W. G., Bate, Mrs. 52. Smith et Filles. 53. Biggs, Albert
(Greengrocer). 54. New Economic Stores (Pipers Penny Bazaar). 55.

Palmer G. H. 56. Spencer's Radio Shop. 59–61. Turner, A. T. (Ladies Wear) Fleece Inn (Grove, H. E.) 62. Ellis, T. P. (Cakes). 64. Gwynne, B. (Fruiterer). 66. Smout and Son. 67. Lipton Ltd. (Grocer). 68. Cassell, E. and Son. (Tailors) 70. Hughes Ltd. 71. Brown, W. and W. (Coal Merchants). 72. Premier Wallpaper Stores. 73. Millar, J. and R.

Plymouth Chambers: More Eva. Liverpool Victoria Insurance Office. First Church of Christ Scientist. Fourt, M. Bevan, A. The National Clothing and Supply Company Ltd. Stanley, G. H. C. and Company. Robinson, J. 74. Bosworth, V. W. Pitts (Redditch) Ltd. 75. Borough Building Society. 76. Avery, J. R. 76. Bayliss, A. J. 77. Grant and Company. 78. Avery, G. 79. Alcester Co-operative Society. 81. Holifields, C. (Draper). 83. Hawkeswood, G. H. (Butcher). 85. Alcester Co-operative Society. 86. Sealey, P. W. 87. Barnwell and Son. 88. Turner, W. D. 89. Millward, S. (Grocer). 90. Margaret Wool Shop. 91. Leach, E. F. 92. Express Valet Service. Blackford Charles. 94. James, Mollie. 95. The Brewery. 97–107. Alcester Co-operative Shops. 101. Hawkeswood Geo. 102. Layton Electric Company Ltd. 104. Andrews, Cecil. 106. Vale, Thomas 108. Trout, Mrs. 109. Fountain, W. H. 110. Chambers, J. 111. Smith, E. M. 112. Biggs, Frank. 113. Wells, Mrs. 114. Danks, E. 115. Webb, Mrs E. 116. Lister, W. 118. Layton, Ellen. 119. Maunton, W. (Furniture) Gospel Hall. 120. Facer, L. G. 123. Dingley, C. L. 124. Williams, T. A. and Sons. 125. Danks, H. 126. Davis, Mrs. 127. Coleman, R. 133. Bartleet, A. 134. Lewis, Ernest. 136. Mutton, E. J. 138. Mole, D. H. 142. Lazell, A. E. 145. Crane, J. E. 147. Humphries, E. G. 148. Hill, C. 157. Mutton, D. J. 159. James, F. H. 161. Kendall, H. Plough and Harrow Hotel (Sollis, F. W.). 165. Tolley, W.

Kathleen Place: 1. Harber, R. 2. Humphries, A. 3. Parry, Mrs. 4. James, F. W. 6. Vale, H.
Unicorn Hill: 2. Hepworth Ltd. 3. Bratley, R. W. 4. Collins Bros. (Butchers). 6. Garfield, A. 7. Green's. Loveday, Smith and Perrins. 8. Whiteman, J. Unicorn Hotel (K. Fowler). Cox, H. P. Rice Misses (Flowers, Fruit) 9. Davis, Mrs W. Ashfield, Mrs cl. h2. Day, Mrs E. clh1. 14. Ryder, A. H. 19. Harrison, T. G. 20. Rowlands. N. R. Service Laundries. 23. Mullin, John. 25. Day, Alice. 26. Lawley, B. 27. Crooke, Bert. 28. Styles, F. 29. Charman, K. E. and M. 31. Day, A. 33. Hack, R. 35. Yates, A. E. 37. Chambers, Alfred. 39. Ross, Mrs Annie. 41. Worcestershire Model Laundry. 42. Crow, E. and Sons. 43. Wilmore Lily. 44. Wheeler, J. and Son. 45. Merry, Frank. 46. Williams, S. 47. Harris, R. 48. Jones Harold Ltd (Coal). 49. Cox, T. H. 50. Mutton,

G. F. 51. Cleveley, H. 53. Johnson, Mrs. 54. Barratt, H. J. 56. Crow, T. 58. Long, Mrs E. 64. Shrimpton and Mobberley. 67. Maries, R. The Redditch Garages Ltd. 62. Britannic Assurance Co. Ltd. Maison Stanley. The Redditch Coal and Coke Co. Ltd. Railway Inn (Tunks Wm) Wright John and Sons Station Yard. 66. Sandilands, J. 70. Davis, J. Halifax Building Society Central Chambers. Lambert, G. F. Central Chambers. Redditch Land Development Co. Ltd. Harrison Charles and Son. Fountain, G. A. Redditch Pure Milk Company Ltd. Thomas George. Hemming Thos. F. and Son. Whiteley and Pickering. Yates, E. J. Redditch and District Commercial Travellers' Association. Unicorn Hotel. Redditch Rugby Football Club, Unicorn Hotel.

Church Green East: 3. White Charles, T. 4. Peart, Mrs C. M. 5. Adams, Mrs. 6. Smallwood Hospital Board Room and Office. "Beech House". 7 and 8. Gold, T. N. 8a. Webb, E. B. 9. Andrews, J. and Son. 10. Green, W. and G. 11. Auction, Mart. 12. Tarleton, H. B. 13. Powell, Mrs. 14. Harbon, G. H. 15. Styler, J. H. 16a. Bowen, W. J. W. 17. Davis, A. E. Lloyds Bank Ltd. 18. East Worcestershire Water Works Company. 20. Webb, E. T. and Sons. Webb, Miss Ethel. 21. Jackson, C. 22. Dyer and Davis. 22a. Harris John S. 22a. Brazil, Alice. 23. Smith, Misses. 24. Smith, T. 24. Wilson, Dr George.

Church Green West: 1. Alabaster, E. B. Joscelyne, H. P. Fisher, H. G. Joscelyne Miss, T. 2. Bawcutt (chemist) Redditch Gas Showrooms. Boyd, L. H. 6. Ellis, T. P. (Cafe and Cake Shop). 7a. Buckley. 7. Wilshaw's. Midland Bank Ltd. Redditch Benefit Building Society. Smallwood Hospital.

Church Road, Redditch: Kerwood, Hobson, Thomas and Company. (Solicitors). 7. Wyers, Miss. Neasom and White (auctioneers). General Post Office. Public Reading Room. Lewis, A. D. Gaumont Palace. Ambulance Station. Midland "Red" Bus Company. Police Station. Ministry of Labour. Whitehouse L and B. The Wakefield Manufacturing Company. 25. Guise, Harry. 27. Green, J. R. 26. Griffin, W. H. (C. S. M.) Drill Hall 8th Bn. Worcestershire Rgt. 29. Lamb, H. 31. Hughes, E. 33. Phipps, Miss, Mogg R. County Council Infant Welfare Centre.

Clarke's Yard: (off Alcester Street). 1. Crook, Mrs. 2. Whitehouse, C. 3. Field, Charles. 4. Rider, A. 5. Hill, G. 6. Long, J. 7. Townsend, W.

Prospect Hill: Mr Brisband. County Court Registrar. Neasom, Mrs "Red House". 2. Barnsley, O. 3. Potts, Dr. C. L. 4. Ames, James. 5. Neale, H. V. 6. Adams and Son. 8. Gray, O. 9. Eleanor Madame. (Hairdresser) Redditch Firewood Company. Hill's Yard. Cottrell and Son. Hill's Yard. Post Office Engineering dept, Hill's Yard. 12. Pitts Elizabeth, M. 13. Birch, F. 14. Baylis, W. V. 15. Pettifer, J. 16. Burns, Dr. N. C. 17. Jones Min. 18. Edwards, R. A. 19. Sykes and Mullins. Wyers, C. and Sons. Redditch Social Service Club, Prospect House. Eades, A. Hemming's Entry. Turner, S. and Son. Maries and Coulson. Forge Factory. Clarkes (Redditch) Ltd. 20. Smith, F. W. 23. Bunegar, Miss. 24. Baylis, H. 25. Milligan, C. 26. Thornton, W. A. 27. Hill, C. W. 31. Hill, Mrs Hubert. 32. Haywood, Emily. 36. Perkins, W. 38. Lee, C. F. 40. Ward, F. C. 42. Ellis, Louisa. 44. Hughes, J. 46. Dolphin, F. P. 47. Blick, Frederick. 48. Sealey, A. 49. Davis, Mrs Ralph, H. W. "Tregantle". 50. Boycott, T. 51. Davis, T. H. 52. Jones, Arthur. 53. Cotton, T. 54. Crow, B. and Son. 54a. Griffin, C. H. 54b. Hemming, Mrs. 55. Allmark, Jos. 56. Clarkson, O. 57. Painter, James. 58. Mrs Ansell. 59. Davis, Mrs. 60. Dyson, Mrs. 62. Gallaway, J. 63. Clarke, J. J. 64. Samman, W. 66. Croughton, H. Ludford, Mrs "The Willows". 80. Clarke, Mrs. British Mills. Harris, G. C. and S. W. and S. Power Company Sub-Station. The Prymware Hosiery Company. Premier Fishing Tackle Company. Huins James Ltd.

AERIAL VIEW OF THE KINGFISHER SHOPPING CENTRE, REDDITCH

General Directory for Webheath. 1934.

Webheath Hall Bowling Club: Sec. and Treas: Mr W Unitt, 66, Heathfield Road.
Village Hall, Heathfield Road. Hon. Sec. and Treas: J. C. F. Morson.
Caretaker: Mrs E Browning, Heathfield Road.
Church of St Philip: Curate: Rev: P. R. Pleming. The Parsonage, Webheath.
Baptist Chapel: Branch of the Redditch Baptist Church.

Adcock, A. Crumpfields Lane.
Allcock, Mrs Fl 44, Birchfield Road
Allcock, Charles. Spring Vale.
Andrews, Mrs J. Andrews. 122, Heathfield Road.
Andrews, Miss. Foxlydiate Hill.
Annis, G. Brownless Farm. Hill Top
Appleyard, George. The Cottage.
Austin, H. 315, Birchfield Road.

Ballard, Mrs. Vincent Farm.
Bakewell, Arthur. 67, Heathfield Road.
Barber, Edward 134. Heathfield Road.
Barker, Reuben. 39. Heathfield Road.
Bartlam, Henry. Pump House Farm.
Batty, T. Grocer Heathfield Road.
Baylis, Sidney. 84, Heathfield Road.
Baylis, H. W. Baylis. 275, Bromsgrove Road.
Betterton, F. Birchfield Road.
Badger, H. 120, Heathfield Road.
Badger, W. A. 105, Heathfield Road.
Bint, W. E. Foxlydiate.
Bluck Bros. Coal Dealers. Pumphouse Lane.
Bonham, T. Farmer. Hill Top.
Boulton, C. W. 319, Birchfield Road.
Boulton, E. G. Hill Top.
Boulton, O. W. 7, Woodside Avenue. Birchfield Road.
Brae, E. W. 119, Heathfield Road.
Brown, A. C. 289, Birchfield Road.
Brown William. Birchfield Road.
Browning, Charles. 54, Heathfield Road.
Browning, Mrs 99, Heathfield Road.
Browning, Miss 48, Heathfield Road.
Browning, J. Crumpfields Lane.
Browning, S. jun. Heathfield Road.
Bryan, G. 275, Birchfield Road.
Bryan, Albert. 116, Heathfield Road.
Bryant, G. Lewisvale. Hill Top.
Buckley. Thos. Sheltwood Farm.
Bunegar. Mrs Foxlydiate. Burdett, F. J. 94, Heathfield Road.
Farmer. R. Springhill Farm.

Carr, Reuben Walter. Hill Top.
Carter, H. 391, Birchfield Road.
Carwardine, Mrs J. 138, Heathfield Road.
Cater, E. W. 78 Heathfield Road.
Chambers, A. G. Council Houses. Hill Top.
Chambers, C. Heathfield Road.
Chambers, J. H. Birchfield Road.

Chambers, Mrs E. Pumphouse Lane.
Chatterley, Mrs E. 23, Heathfield Road.
Collier, E. A. Birchfield Road.
Cook, F. 5, Woodside Avenue. Birchfield Road.
Compton, Mrs E. Upper Norgrove.
Compton, Miss M. Upper Norgrove.
Cooper, W. 71, Heathfield Road.
Cope, Mrs W. 403, Birchfield Road.
Cottrill, R. 88, Heathfield Road.
Court, Joseph. 42, Heathfield Road.
Court, Mrs E. 42, Heathfield Road.
Court, W. A. 9, Heathfield Road.
Cox, George. 63, Heathfield Road.
Cox, Wallace. Spring Vale.
Craner, W. E. 65, Heathfield Road.
Creed, L. 277, Birchfield Road.
Cresswell. Crumpfields Lane.
Cresswell, O. Crumpfields Lane.

Davis, J. H. 59, Heathfield Road.
Davis, Florence. 55, Heathfield Road.
Davis, E. 119, Heathfield Road.
Davis, G. 40, Heathfield Road.
Davis, J. T. 57, Heathfield Road.
Davis, Mrs 59, Heathfield Road.
Davis, Mrs 135, Birchfield Road.
Dawe, W. E. 111, Heathfield Road.
Diggins, A. E. Crumpfields Lane.
Dipple, Mrs S. Pumphouse Lane.
Dobbs, C. H. 130, Heathfield Road.
Dodd, T. Hill Top.
Dolphin, P. The Heath, Heathfield Road.
Dolton, H. 385, Birchfield Road.
Drew, Mrs T, Hill Top.
Drover, A. 50, Heathfield Road.
Dyde, E. Foxlydiate.
Dyde, J. Foxlydiate.
Dyde, Samuel, G. Foxlydiate.
Dyer, Mrs 56, Heathfield Road.

English, G. T. Foxlydiate.
Evans, W. E. D. Fox and Goose Inn. Foxlydiate.

Farley, W. F. Pumphouse Lane.
Farr, George. Foxlydiate.
Farr, James. 35, Heathfield Road.
Field, R. Crumpfields Lane.
Field, L. 136, Heathfield Road.
Finch, A. 2, Woodside Avenue. Birchfield Road.
Fletcher, Mrs 32, Heathfield Road.

Fletcher, T. A. 72, Heathfield Road.
Foster, F. 305, Birchfield Road.
Foster, Mrs Park Cottages. Hewell.
Fowler, T. R. 1, Heathfield Road.
Frost, W. H. 63, Heathfield Road.
Fryer, John. L. 73, Heathfield Road.
Fulwell, Frank. 25, Heathfield Road.

Gardner, G. J. 128, Heathfield Road.
Gibbs, Arthur. 85, Heathfield Road.
Goode, W. Coal Dealer. Hill Top.
Goulbourne, A. J. Tack Farm.
Green, F. Hill Top.
Green, J. G. The Gables. Webheath.
Green, Mrs 68, Heathfield Road.
Griffin, Thomas. 44, Heathfield Road.
Griffin, Frank. 41, Heathfield Road.
Farmer, T. 109, Heathfield Road.

Hands, J. 323, Birchfield Road.
Harris, G. 117, Heathfield Road.
Harrison, N. C. Cornah. Crumpfields Lane.
Harvey, Misses. Bank's Green.
Harvey, William. Bank's Green.
Harman, David. 97, Heathfield Road.
Harman, Mrs 26, Heathfield Road.
Harris, Mrs 95, Heathfield Road.
Harris, G. Hy. Hill Top.
Harris, W. Pumphouse Lane.
Hawkeswood, H. 309, Birchfield Road.
Hawthorne, G. 335, Birchfield Road.
Hawthorne, T. 6, Woodside Avenue. Birchfield Road.
Heath, T. Plasterer. Hill Top.
Hemus, J. 3, Woodside Avenue. Birchfield Road.
Hill, H. P. Springhill Farm.
Hillman, G. Pumphouse Lane.
Hims, H. Crumpfields Lane.
Hims, Claude. Crest Garage. Crumpfields Lane.
Hims, Bros. Crumpfields Farm.
Hodgetts, A. 311, Birchfield Road.
Hodgetts, F. 313, Birchfield Road.
Hodgetts, H. Heathfield Road.
Hopkins, C. Pumphouse Lane.
Horton, G. 295, Birchfield Road.
Huins. "Westcroft" Birchfield Road.
Hughes, G. Council Houses. Hill Top.
Hughes, Richard. Farmer. Foxlydiate.
Hughes, W. H. 15, Heathfield Road.
Hulland, T. A. 30, Heathfield Road.
Hulland, Wilfred. 132, Heathfield Road.
Humphries, H. Post Office. Foxlydiate.
Hunt, C. 51, Heathfield Road.
Huntley, B. J. Crumpfields Lane.
Hurley, W. H. S. 77, Heathfield Road.

Jackson, Fred. 93, Heathfield Road.
James, A. C. 47, Heathfield Road.
James, Albert. 101, Heathfield Road.
James, Alfred, C. 72, Heathfield Road.
James, A. C. 95, Heathfield Road.

James, Mrs F. 113, Heathfield Road.
James, Mrs J. Birchfield Road.
James, Thos. 27, Heathfield Road.
Jeffs, H. Pumphouse Lane.
Jarvis, F. Park View. Birchfield Road.
Jervis, Frank. Birchfield Road.
Johnson, A. Hill Top.
Johnson, A. 46, Heathfield Road.
Johnson, S. 61, Heathfield Road.
Jones, Herbert. 81, Heathfield Road.
Jones, Thomas. 86, Heathfield Road.

Keyte, H. 307, Birchfield Road.
Knight, H. A. 118, Heathfield Road.
Knight, Wm. D. 28, Heathfield Road.
Lambley, M. A. 47, Heathfield Road.

Langston, F. H. Birchfield Road.
Langston, Mrs E. 140, Heathfield Road.
Layton, Wm. 308, Birchfield Road.
Layton, Wm. E. Birchfield Road.
Leaman, F. J. 126, Heathfield Road.
Lee, B. Shopkeeper and Post Office. Foxlydiate.
Lee, E. 29, Heathfield Road.
Lee, J. 401, Birchfield Road.
Lee, W. F. 107, Heathfield Road.
Lewis, Mrs "Redcroft" Birchfield Road.
Lewis, W. 34, Heathfield Road.
Lowe, A. W. Crumpfields Lane.

Maisey, F. 19, Heathfield Road.
Melley, Fred. 13, Heathfield Road.
Mitchell, J. A. 395, Birchfield Road.
McCandlish, L. Foxlydiate House.
Moore, H. 37, Heathfield Road.
Moore, T. 64, Heathfield Road.
Moore, W. 301, Birchfield Road.
Morrall, H. Birchfield Road.
Morrell, Mrs 94, Heathfields Road.

Nash, H. W. 104, Heathfield Road.
Nicholson, G. 117, Heathfield Road.
Nicholls, Mrs 5, Pumphouse Lane.

Oliver, Mrs 339, Birchfield Road.
Owen, J. Hill Top.

Palmer, Captain. Crumpfield Lane.
Palmer, G. H. 80, Heathfield Road.
Palmer, Mrs W. Green Lanes Farm.
Parsons, E. I. 387, Birchfield Road.
Parsons, Edgar. Pumphouse Lane.
Partridge, D. 83, Heathfields Road.
Perks, Joseph. 60, Heathfield Road.
Perks, Arthur. 52, Heathfield Road.
Perkins, A. E. 69, Heathfield Road.
Perkins, G. 114, Heathfield Road.
Perry, H. W. 399, Birchfield Road.
Peterson, E. 115, Heathfield Road.
Philips, James. 92, Heathfield Road.
Pitcher Police-constable. Lewisvale. Hill Top.
Platts, George, G. Old Paper Mill.

Preedy, W. Heathfield Road.
Pleming, Rev. P. R. Church Road.
Portman, A. 74, Heathfield Road.

Read, F. G. 70, Heathfield Road.
Read, H. Springvale.
Rendle, C. F. "Kenwyn" Crumpfields Lane.
Rice, F. Crumpfields Lane.
Robinson, G. W. Hill Top.
Robinson, J. Ed. 79, Heathfield Road.
Robinson, W. T. 75, Heathfield Road.
Rodgers, Mrs 4, Woodside Avenue. Birchfield Road.
Rudge, Bros. Birch Tree Farm. Birchfield Road.

Savery, George. 389, Birchfield Road.
Scott, J. The Cove. Crumpfields Lane.
Sealey, A. 397, Birchfield Road.
Sealey Edgar. Foxlydiate.
Sealey, E. L. Crumpfields Lane.
Sealey, George. 76b, Heathfield Road.
Sealey, George Fred. Hill Top.
Sessions, F. W. 111b. Heathfield Road.
Sharpe, V. R. 92, Heathfield Road.
Sheppard, W. Baker. Heathfield Road.
Small, Levi. 62, Heathfield Road.
Smallwood, J. Crumpfields Lane.
Smith, A. E. 293, Bromsgrove Road.
Smith, Sydney. 269, Bromsgrove Road.
Smith, J. Birchfield Road.
Stanley, E. E. 121, Heathfield Road.
Stanley, George. Spring Hill.
Stanley, Reuben. 24, Heathfield Road.
Stewart, Harold, O. 1, Woodside Avenue. Birchfield Road.
Spiers, C. Hy. 21, Heathfield Road.
Spiers, G. D. 90, Heathfield Road.
Stoddard, James. Foxlydiate.
Swinbourne, G. A. 45, Heathfield Road.
Swinbourne, W. A. Spring Hill.

Tarplee, Mrs 103, Heathfield Road.
Taylor, E. Birchfield Road.
Taylor, E. M. Heathfield Road.
Tongue, J. Lanehouse Farm. Foxlydiate.
Tongue, H. J. Pumphouse Farm.
Tipping, F. 84, Heathfield Road.
Turner, A. C. 81, Heathfield Road.
Turner, A. E. Sycamore Farm. Heathfield Road.
Twigg, Walter. 31, Heathfield Road.

Unitt, W. 66, Heathfield Road.

Vann, J. Dairyman. Crumpfields Lane.
Vann, Mrs. Rose and Crown Inn. Webheath.

Walker, A. B. Box Knot Farm. Heathfield Road.
Walker, A. B. 271, Birchfield Road.
Wall, A. 53, Heathfield Road.
Walmsley, F. H. 271, Birchfield Road.
Wanklin, T. 58, Heathfield Road.
Ward, A. 17, Heathfield Road.

While, D. 96, Heathfield Road.
White, E. Crumpfields Lane.
While, H. Grocer and Post Office. Heathfield Road.
Wiggett, Charles. Hill Top.
Wilkes, R. A. 113, Heathfield Road.
Wormington, J. W. 337, Birchfield Road.
Wormington, Philip. Foxlydiate.
Wright, W. Birchfield Road.

Yapp, William. General Stores. 123, Heathfield Road.
Yoxall, Mrs 49, Heathfield Road.

Local people and places

Robinson, E. 7, Adelaide Street.
Ross, E. Clarke's Yard.
Rowley, Benjamin. 6, Pound Yard.
Russell, A. Leah Place. 87, Prospect Road.
Sage, J. R. Draper. 2, Bates Hill.
Satchwell, T. 3, Charles Street.
Scott, J. and Company. Draper. Market Place.
Sealey, Ernest. Holloway Lane.
Shakespeare, E. General Dealer. George Street.
Slade, H. Margaret Place. Queen Street.
Smart, Mrs. 10, Smallwood's Row, Peakman Street.
Smart, Mrs. Gorton Arch. Smallwood's Row.
Smith, John. Webheath Lane. Webheath.
Southwick, Clive. 3, Charles Street.
Spooner, A. 23, Skinner's Buildings.
Strain, Arthur Junior. Beoley Cottages.
Street, E. Parson's Row.
Styler, Arthur. Marlpit Lane.
Sutton, B. 14, Bates Hill.
Swann, G. 11, Silver Street.
Talbot, William. Pound Yard.
Taylor, H. 2, Grove's Square. Walford Street.
Taylor, Mrs. Hill Street.
Terry, George. 1. Izod's Yard. (Front Hill) Evesham Street.
Tolley, S. 3, Union Street.
Tolley, Mrs T Sen: Skinner's Buildings. George Street.
Tongue, F. 93, Robinson's Yard.
Treadgold, R. 97, St George's Road.
Vale, S. Back 1. Alcester Street.
Vaughan, W. 3, Grove's Buildings. Walford Street.
Walton, Alfred. 8, Silver Street.
Waring, B. Junior. 5, Kathleen Place. Evesham Street. Front Hill.
Wedgbury, F. 15, Skinner Street.
Smith, Parsons Row. Mount Pleasant.
Carr, J. 121, Harris's Lane.

Streets and local Tradesmen:

Mrs Haden. back of 45, Unicorn Hill,
James, Hall, Council buildings, Beoley Road,

George, Henry Hanson, Tin, Smith. 10, Unicorn Hill.
Harber, R. Kathleen Place, off Evesham Street.
Harding, F. W. Tobacconist. 16, Bates Hill.
Harris, Mrs. 44a, Holloway Lane.
Harrison, J. 2, Smallwood Row.
Hawkeswood, W. 25, Skinners Buildings.
Hayward, Samuel, Almshouses.
Heaphy and Sons. Tailors, New Street.
Hearn, Mrs. 9, Izods Yard, Evesham Street.
Heath, F. G. Salisbury House, Mount Pleasant.
Hewitt, F. Chapel Street.
Higgs, Henry. Butcher. 42, Alcester Street.
Hill, Percy. Littleworth. Park Road.
Hill, Eli. Herbert Square, George Street.
Hill, George. Clarke's Yard, Alcester Street.
Hill, Miss. 8, Church Green East.
Hodgetts, W. Parsons Row, Mount Pleasant.
Holliday, John. Muscatt's Way.
Hollington, John. Bridge Street.
Hollis, G. Archer Road.
Holmes, Walter. 2, Ipsley Row.
Hopkins, F. Hook Manufacturer. "Brooklyn" Rectory Road.
Horne, Charles. Brockhill Lane.
Horton, M. Ivor Road.
Hough, W. 7, Smallwoods Row.
Houghton, G. 6, Salters Lane.
Hughes, P. Ferney Hill Brickworks.
Huins, James. Market Place.
Huins, Harry. 25, Glover Street.
Humphries, James. 12, Beaufort Street.
Hunt, A. 91, Robinson's Square, Evesham Road.
Hyde, J. Walkwood Lane.
Ireson, W. A. Newsgent. 127, Evesham Road.
Jakeman, W. Forge Mills.
James, Oliver. 3, Hill Street.
Jephcott, J. E. Bromfield Road.
Johnson, J. Phillip's Terrace, Beoley Road.
Knight, Joseph. Silver Street.
Lee, H. 25, Skinner's Buildings, George Street.
Lewis, S. "Sherborne". Feckenham Road.
Locke, Charles. Old Toll Gate.
Mann, W. Stationmaster. Unicorn Hill.
Maries, A. 9, Skinner Street.
Markham, H. "The Nook", Salop Road.
Marshall, T. Town Crier. 3, Victoria Street.
Martin, H. 11, Mason Road.
Mathews, D. Highfields, Headless Cross.
Millward, G. 13, Skinner Street.
Moss, Frederick. Salter's Lane.
National Telephone Company. Church Green East.
Neason, Mrs. Birchensdale Farm. Salter's Lane.
Neasom, S. Lowans Hill.
Newall, L. Charles Street.
Newton, Rev. Canon. "Holmwood".
Palmer, Mrs. 12, Bates Hill.
Palmer, Thomas. Brockhill Lane.
Parker, Walter. "Stowe", Clive Avenue. Birmingham Road.
Pears and Company, Ladies and Children's Outfitters. The Parade.

Peart, E. Ludlow Road.
Petford, T. 2, Katherine Place, Evesham Street.
Pinfield, G. Council Buildings, Beoley Road.
Pipers, Penny Bazaar. Evesham Street.
Purcell, T. 3, Adelaide Street off Bates Hill.
Purcell, Henry. 14, Warwick Place, Ipsley Street.
Read, W. Horsebreaker. Royal Hotel Mews.
Poole Place at the end of Alcester Street.

Factories:
Philip Spencer. Needles, Pins. Ipsley Street and Oswald Street.
Edward White: Engineer. Windsor Works, Redditch.
Frederick Field and Sons: Needle Pointing, Talking Machine Needles. (Gramaphone) Winsor Road.
John Wright and Sons. Timber Merchants. Station Yard. Redditch.
Jonah Warner. Needle Toolmaker and Swivel Manufacturer.
J. and W. Mitchell. Bordesley Paper Works. Birmingham Road.
Royal Enfield. Agent; A. Bell and Company, Market Place.
James Ross, Engineer. Mappleborough Green.
Edward Dyer. Accountant. 22, Church Green East.
Charles Hughes and Son. China, Glass, Etc. Evesham Street Stores.
The Redditch Indicator Company Ltd. New Factory, General Printers. Easemore Road. Built by Mr C. G. Huins.
Holland. Caterer. Bidford-upon-Avon Pleasure Grounds.
Henry Higgs. Butcher. 42, Alcester Street.
Frederick, T. Treadgold. Artist. 270, Mount Pleasant.
A. Myers. Florist. 35, Alcester Street.
William J. Mousley. Chemist. 21, Alcester Street.
Hopkins, G. F. Jeweller. 67, Evesham Street.
Monks, E. D. Files, Rasps Manufacturers. 55, Alcester Street.
Harrison, Cyril H. Builder. Oswald Street.
Llewellyn, W. J. Iron Foundry. Wellington Foundry, Redditch.
Huins and Seden Ltd. F. C. Builders. The Brickworks, Lodge Road, Town Office, Alcester Street.
Ladbury Ernest. Machinist. 40, Alcester Street.
Tongue Edgar. Wheelwright, Cycle and Motor Garage, Coach Builder, Clive Works, Redditch.
Palmer, Cecil. Jeweller. 10, Evesham Street.
Adams, W. H. Swivel and Tackle Manufacturer. Britten Street.
Allcocks, S. and Company. Fish Hook and Tackle Manufacturers. Standard Works, Clive Road.
Allwood, A. and Company. Needle Manufacturers. St Anne's Works, Clive Road.
Avery, A. G. Builder. 88, Evesham Street.

Barker, John H. Needle Finisher to the trade. Clark's Mill.

Bartlett, E. and Company. Tackle Manufacturers. Easemore Road.

Bartlett William and Sons Ltd. Sewing Machine Needles, Crochet Hooks, Fish Hooks and Tackle Manufacturers. Abbey Mills. Established 1750.

Merchants, Shops Restaurants

A. A. Gray. Tobacconists. Picture Framing. The Central Cigar Store. 5, Evesham Street.

White's Restaurant. Unicorn Hill.

Haines, T. and Sons. Tailors. Hunt Tailors, Habit Makers, Military Uniforms, Christy's Hats and Caps. Evesham Street.

Huins, C. G. and Sons. Builders. Pool Place.

Harold Jones. Coal and Coke. 48, Unicorn Hill.

Picture Houses

Bosco's Pictures Ltd. Public Hall. Manager: Mr Ritson.

Picture House. Alcester Street. Proprietoress: Mrs R. Treadgold.

The Redditch Palace Ltd. Alcester Street. Manager: Mr J. Baron.

The Temperance Hotel: 77, Evesham Street. Proprietress: Mrs Ludford.

Ladies Clothes

Fancy Drapery Department. 79, Evesham Street.

Mr Harry B. Tarleton. Builder. Fowl-Houses, Shop Fronts. Ipsley Street.

Philip Spencer and Sons. Surgeons' and other Fancy Needles, Pins. Ipsley and Oswald Street.

F. W. Hollington and Company Ltd. Furniture, Drapery. Evesham Street.

Myers, D. and Sons. Florists. 139, Evesham Street and Holloway Gardens.

Styler, E. Newsagent. 56, Alcester Street.

Treadgold. Draughtsman. 270, Mount Pleasant.

Baylis, E. Furniture Dealer. Oak House, Alcester Street.

Hodges, E. A. Newsagent. 1, Evesham Street. Telephone Number 57.

Redditch Indicator: Stationery Department. 4, Prospect Hill.

Williams, F. Jewellers, Watch and Clock Makers. 54, Alcester Street.

Rose, F. W. Shoeing. Ipsley Street. (Adjoining Messrs. C. G. Huin's Offices).

Farr, G. P. Newsagent. 48, Evesham Street.

Smith, W. H. Car Sales. Open and Closed Cars. 42, Evesham Street.

Humphries, E. G. Butcher. 137, Evesham Street and 4, Alcester Street.

Ashwins. Pipes and Tobaccos. 26, Evesham Street.

Warner, Jonah. Needle Manufacturers. Bromsgrove Road.

Picture House. Bosco's Pictures. 4d and 7d

Children: 2d and 4d. Thoroughly disinfected. Plush, Tip-up Seats.

Scorza and Oliver, Wines and Spirits. 31, Evesham Street. Manager: Mr A. H. Chatterley.

Wilkes, H. Tobacconist. Railway Approach.

Morris, John. Grocer. Evesham Street. Tea 2/8d per pound.

Webb and Sons. Bakers. Church Green.

Sturges, W. J. Scrap Iron Stores, Peakman Street. Office: 20, Mount Pleasant.

Dolphin, F. P. Grocer. Fish Hill House, Redditch.

Willets Bros: Butchers. 18, Evesham Street.

Johnson, Mark. Florist. Church Road and Stall Number 5, Market Place.

Neasom and White. Auctioneers. Church Road.

Morris, F. H. Drapers. Mount Pleasant.

Walmsley, Frank. Tailors. 49, Unicorn Hill. Gents Suits 37/6d. Overcoat 37/6d. Blue, Grey and Brown Nap.

Huntleys. Undertakers. Park Road Mews. Funeral Furnishers.

Bennett, F. L. Musical Dealer. Pianos, Gramaphones. Mount Pleasant.

Beck's Shop. Cobbler. All Shoe Repairs. 16, Alcester Street.

Heath, T. H. D. Furnishers. 84, Evesham Street.

Pears, G. E. and Company. Ladies' and Childrens' Outfitters. The Parade.

Huxley, George. Coffin Maker. Astwood Bank.

Ledbury, John. Window Blind Manufacturers. Wellington Street.

Sarsons, W. E. Baker. Foregate Street, Astwood Bank.

Dyer, John and Sons. Ironmonger, Hardware, Gas Mantles, Lamp Oil. Alcester Street.

Pheonix Assurance Company Ltd. Insurance. Established 1782.

Thompson, B. R. Butcher. 51, Alcester Street.

Gross, James and Son. Florist. 88, Evesham Street.

Thomas, Misses. Bonnets and Wools. 17, Evesham Street.

Knight, T. Coal Dealer. Grange Wharf.

Trout Bros. Bakers. Astwood Bank. Near Motor Bus Terminus.

Sorrell, W. C. Newsagent. Astwood Bank.

Spencer, G. Jeweller. 16, Evesham Street.

Jones, G. W. Butcher. 17, Alcester Street.

Bate, W. George. (Late George Scriven) Glazier. 13, Oswald Street. Shop: 45, Evesham Street.

Steeles. Butcher. 31, Alcester Street.

Shepard, J. Monumental Mason. Ipsley Street.

Tye, Will. Cycle Repairs, Flash-lamps, Gramaphones. Palace Garage. (18 years Foreman at Eadie's Factory and B.S.A. Company.)

Palmer, Cecil. Jeweller. 10, Evesham Street.

Huins Boots. The Boot Metropole. 7/11d and 21/-.

Trout, H. W. Undertaker. New Road, Astwood Bank.

Pitts, A. L. Car Hire. Evesham Street, Redditch.

Feast, William and Sons. Evesham Road, Headless Cross. Tailors: Suits 18/11d, 35/-, 39/- Fitted 75/-.

Frank Walmsley. 49, Unicorn Hill. Ladies' and Gents' Tailors. Perfect Fit Guaranteed. Gents' Suits Made to Measure. 37/6d. Blue Serge. Smart Cashmere. From 40/-. Blue, Grey, Brown Nap Overcoats to Measure 35/-d.

Adcock, The Parade.

Albutt, Misses. Dressmakers. 2, St Georges Road.

Alcester Co-operative Society. Number 5, Branch. Evesham Street.

Amies. Boot Repairs. 34, Evesham Street.

Andrews, J. and Sons. Electricians. Church Green East.

Andrews, G. Tobacconist. Mason Road, Headless Cross.

Avery, Mrs E. Draper. 64, Evesham Street.

Baker, W. Bootmaker. 44, Alcester Street.

Baker, T. Butcher. 21, Mount Pleasant.

Baker, Miss Milliner. 28, Mount Pleasant.

Baker, R. Pork Butcher. Mount Pleasant.

Banks, P. C. Artillery Barracks. Easemore Road.

Barren and Company. Tailors. Evesham Road.

Barrett, J. T. Saddler. Unicorn Hill.

Bate, W. G. Painter and Decorater. 13, Oswald Street.

Bawcutt, F. Chemist. The Parade.

Baylis, H. G. Auctioneer. Church Green West.

Baylis, E. House Furnishers. 49, Alcester Street.

Baylis, T. and Company. Needle and Fish-hook Manufacturer. Beoley Road.

Baylis, S. General Dealer. 41, Hewell Road.

Beck, E. Bootmaker. 16, Alcester Street.

Bell, A. and Company. Music Warehouse and Cycle Agents. 6, Market Place.

Bennett, F. Lewis. Music Warehouse. 42, Mount Pleasant.

Bennett, Miss A. Dressmaker, Other Road.

Bennet, Mrs G. Boxmaker. 1, Peakman Street.

Biggs, Albert. Greengrocer. Market Place and Evesham Street.

Biggs, A. Greengrocer. 43, Archer Road.

Bird, Alfred. Butcher. 149, Evesham Road.

Bladon, Miss Haberdasher. 55, Evesham Street.

Bladon, W. Insurance Agent. 9, Park Road.

Boarding House. The Shrubbery, Prospect Hill. Proprietress: Mrs Blackford.

Bonaker, G. Baker. 14, Red Lion Street.

Booker, Alfred. Needle and Fishing-tackle Manufacturer. Hewell Road.

Boots Cash Chemist. Evesham Street.

Borough of Birmingham Loan Society. Unicorn Hotel.

Boyd, Mrs Mudie's Library. Church Green West.

Bridge, H. Blacksmith. Evesham Road.

Brough, G. F. Outfitter. 11, Evesham Street.

Borough, Misses. Costumiers. 7, Evesham Street.

Brown, W. and W. Ltd. Corn Merchants. Evesham Street.

Bryant, Miss. Grammar School, Broxwood House, Bromsgrove Road.

Bullock, W. Grocer. 1, Mount Street.

Canning, A. Blacksmith. Red Lion Street and Ipsley Street.

Capital and Counties Bank. Ltd. Church Green East. Manager: Mr R. J. Miller.

Carr, A. E. Bootmaker. 86, Evesham Road.

Cash, J. Farmer. Brockhill Farm, Birchensdale.

Cashmore, W. Grocer. Birchfield Road.

Cassell, E. Clothier. Evesham Street.

Charman, G. Baker. 89, Birchfield Road.

Chinn, C. Greengrocer. 1 and 2, Highfield Road.

Chinn, H. Fishmonger. 151, Evesham Road.

Clement, Mrs. Confectioners. 2, Prospect Road.

Clevelly, H. Golf House, Plymouth Road.

Clews, G. Fishmonger. Prospect Road.

Collins, C. Tailor. 40, Mount Pleasant.

Collins. Pork Butchers. 4, Unicorn Hill.

Cooke, E. Grocer. 148, Evesham Road.

Cooper, A. H. Shoeing Forge. Church Road.

Court, Mrs. Dressmaker. Melen Street.

Court, Mrs M. Confectioner. Ludlow Road.

Cox, H. P. Shoemaker. Unicorn Hill.

Crane and Son. File Makers. 105, Ipsley Street.

Cranmore Simmonds and Company Ltd. Furnishers. Evesham Street.

Crow, T. Coal Merchants. 28, Oakly Road.

Crow, E. and Sons. Grocers. Unicorn Hill.

Crow, Harold. Old Mill Dairy. Windsor Road.

Crow, W. Painter. Easemore Road.

Cund, J. B. Insurance Agent. 160, Evesham Road.

Dale Forty and Company. 7, Church Green West.

Daniels, Mrs A. Greengrocer. 91, Evesham Road.

Daniels, H. Poultry Breeder. 44, Birchfield Road.

Davies, H. Rigby. Draper. 19, Evesham Street.

Davis, H. T. Grocer. Beoley Road.

Davis. Butcher. Evesham Road.

Davis, Miss H. Coaldealer. 41, Melen Street.

Davis, E. and Company. 16a, Park Road.

Davis, Mrs. Dressmaker. 135, Evesham Road.

Davis, William. 17, Church Green East.

Davis, E. Decorater. 55, Evesham Road.

Dawkins, G. Grocer, etc. 90, Evesham Street.

Deakin, John. Butcher. Market Place.

Deaner, W. Shoemaker. 1, William Street.

Dixon, T. and M. Coal Merchants. Hewell Road.

Dobbins, Mrs G. Dressmaker. Clive Road.

Dobbins, W. H. Grocer. 20, Bates Hill.

Dolphin, F. P. Grocer. Fish Hill House.

Dolton. 78, Rectory Road.

Donald, F. Bookbinder. Easemore Road.

Duggins, E. Draper, etc. Unicorn Hill.

Duggins, Mrs. Grocer. 126, Beoley Road.

Duggins, William. Palm Maker. 103, Beoley Road.

Dyer, J. Ironmonger, Cycle Agent. 33, Alcester Street.

Dyer, E. Auctioneer. 22, Church Green East.

Dyson, J. and Company. Tackle Manufacturers. Standard Works, Albert Street.

East Worcestershire Waterworks Company. Church Green East. Collector. Mr W. Lowe.

Eastmans Ltd. Meat Stores. 27, Evesham Street.

Eaves. 127, Evesham Street.

Edkins, W. and Sons. Builders. Saw Mills. Red Lion Street.

Elliot, J. R. Collector of Taxes. 38, Easemore Road.

Enfield Cycle and Motor Works. Hewell Road.

English, J. and Sons. Needle and Sewing Machine Needle Manufacturers. Queen Street.

English, F. and P. Ltd. Manufacturers Spokes for Cycle and Motor Trade. Continental Works.

Evans, F. The Parade.

Evans, T. Educational Publisher. Worcester Road.

Farr, Alfred. Central Buildings. Evesham Road.

Farr, A. and Sons. Needle Manufacturers. Park Road.

Farr, E. Newsagent and Tobacconist. 48, Evesham Street.

Farr, W. Chimney Sweep. 8, Silver Street.

Feast, W. Draper. 131, Evesham Road.

Feasey. Needlemaker. Hewell Road.

Field, Frederick and Son. Needle Pointers. Old Central Pointing Mill.

Field, Charles. Scrap Iron. Silver Street.

Fisher's Sweet Stores. Post Office. Mount Pleasant.

Fitlesons' Bazaar. Alcester Street.

Fletcher, Thomas W. Easemore Farm.

Fletcher, C. B. and Company. Fishing Rod Manufacturers. "Eclipse Works" Hewell Road.

Fox, F. Baker. 3 House 4 Court, Britten Street.

Free. The Saddler. Church Green East.

Freeman, J. Cooper. 30, Worcester Road.

French, F. Shopkeeper. Birchfield Road.

French, Herbert. Weight's Farm.

Galbraith, George. Grocer. 62, Prospect Road.

Galbraith, G. Lloyds Bank.

Gardener, N. Florist. Central Buildings, Evesham Road.

Garfield, B. Boxmaker. Queen Street.

Gas Company Offices. 89, Evesham Street. Showroom for Gas Fires, etc.

Gas Works and Secretary's Office. Birmingham Road.

General Post Office. Church Road.

German and Webb. Tailors. 5, Market Place.

Gibbons, A. Hardener. 20, Grange Road.

Gibbs, W. and Son. Ironmongers. Evesham Street.

Goodwin, J. 76, Evesham Street.

Gold, John A. Veterinary Surgeon. Church Green.

Golf Links. Soudan. Plymouth Road.

Gorin, Mrs. Greengrocer. 2, Alcester Street.

Gray, A. A. Wholesale Tobacconists. 5, Evesham Street.

Grey, E. Drapers. Market Place.

Greaves, W. Fish Fryer. Beoley Road.

Green, S. Hairdresser. Beoley Road.

Green, G. Entertainer. 3, Ludlow Road.

Green, S. G. The Garage, Easemore Road.

Griffiths, L. Fishmonger. 8, Evesham Street.

Griffiths and Company. Furriers. 40, Evesham Street.

Gwynne, B. Fruiterers. Evesham Street.

Hadley, R. Insurance Agent. 138, Evesham Road.

Haines, T. and Sons. Tailors. Evesham Street.

Hall, W. The Garage. Evesham Road.

Hands and Johnson. Draper. Birchfield Road.

Hanson, Tom. Tinsmith. 10, Unicorn Hill.

Harbon, Misses. Osborne House School, Grove Street.

Harding, F. W. Tobacconist. 16, Bates Hill.

Harman and Locke. Photographs. 10, Evesham Road.

Harris, Mrs E. Milliner. 18, Marsden Road.

Harris, A. L. Newsagent. Unicorn Hill.

Harrison, F. G. Grocers. Unicorn Hill.

Hawkeswood, J. Butcher. 83, Evesham Street.

Hawkeswood, E. Butcher. Birchfield Road.

Hawkins, T. Chimney Sweep. Edward Street.

Hawkins, S. Parish Clerk. Ipsley Street.

Hawthorne, B. School House, Peakman Street.

Hayes, Miss E. Dressmaker. 11, Wellington Street.

Heaphy, G. and Sons. Tailors, etc. New Street off Evesham Street.

Heath, T. H. D. House Furnishers. Evesham Street.

Hemming, F. Fruiterers. Unicorn Hill.

Hemming, Miss. Dressmaker. Oswald Street.

Hensman, J. J. Photographs. 5, Church Green East.

Hepworth's. Clothiers. Unicorn Hill.

Higgs, Henry. Butcher. 42, Alcester Street.

Hill, Mrs M. A. Grocers, etc. 29, George Street.

Hill, C. Fish Shop. 94, Evesham Road.

Hill, Percy. Tailor. Littleworth. Park Road.

Hill, Gas Fitter. Ipsley Street.

Hill, Miss. 8, Church Green East.

Hill, Thomas. Bootmaker. 114, Mount Pleasant.

Hill, W. H. Decorator. 53, Alcester Street.

Hilton's Booteries. Unicorn Hill.

Hobson, Thomas and Company. Solicitor. Council East.

Hobbs, J. Boot Repairer. 151, Evesham Road.

Hodges, E. A. Stationer and Newsagent. 1, Evesham Street.

Hollington, F. W. and Company Ltd. Drapers. Evesham Street.

Holloway, Mrs. Grocer. 14, Grove Street.

Home and Colonial Stores. 36, Evesham Street.

Hopkins, A. C. Hairdresser. 16, Market Place.

Hopkins, G. F. Watchmaker. Evesham Street.

Houghton, Misses. Dressmaker. 87, Mount Pleasant.

Hughes, P. Ferney Hill Brickworks, Bromsgrove Road.

Hughes, A. Tobacconist. 11, Alcester Street.

Hughes. Furniture Dealers. Evesham Street Stores.

Hughes, T. C. and Sons. 11, Peakman Street.

Huins, James. Boot and Shoe Factory. Market Place.

Huins, F. C. and Seden. Brickworks, Lodge Road.

Huins, T. Boot Repairers. 13, Beoley Road.

Hulland, S. Baker. 82, Evesham Road, Headless Cross.

Humphries, E. G. Butcher. 137, Evesham Street and 4, Alcester Street.

Humphries, W. Boot Factor. 39, Evesham Street.

Huntley, B. J. Undertakers. 22, Park Road Mews. Park Road.

Hurst. Sweeps. Archer Road.

Lock, Charles. Old Toll Gate. Birmingham Road.

James, F. W. Confectioners. Market Place. (Successors Taylor and Tilley).

James, Mrs. Church Green East.

James, A. Grocer. 18, Beoley Road.

Jarvis, W. H. M. Rate Collector. Council Offices, Evesham Street.

Jarvis, Henry. 10, Church Green East.

Jarvis, Walter and Company. Coal Merchants. 7, Archer Road.

Johnson, J. S. Greengrocer. 34, Alcester Street.

Johnson Bros. Dyers. 15, Evesham Street.

Johnson, Harry. Sweet Stores. 65, Evesham Street.

Johnson. Bootmaker. 10, Mount Pleasant.

St Stephen's School, Peakman Street. Built 1845. Demolished 1983.

Public Houses

Vine Inn. Demolished 1920. Afterwards The Talbot Inn.

The Royal George. Evesham Street. (Afterwards Rainscourt's Faggot Shop).

The Fleece.

The White Swan.

The Rifleman Inn. Maries, G. F. Park Road.

Sportsman Inn. Clements, H. H. Peakman Street.

Crown Hotel. Edwards, R. Prospect Hill.

Queen's Head. Glover, G. H. Queen Street.

Red Lion Inn. Atkins, S. Red Lion Street.

White Lion Inn. Moss, F. H. Red Lion Street.

Railway Hotel. Unicorn Hill.

Unicorn Hotel. Benjamin Brown. Unicorn Hill.

Plumbers Arms. Duffin, A. Walford Street.

Shakespeare Inn. (Closed 1900).

The Lamp. Walford Street. (Closed 1920).

The Eagle. Headless Cross.

The Brockhill Public House. Batchley Estate.

The Rose and Crown. Heathfield Road. Webheath.

Fox and Goose. Foxlydiate. Old Bromsgrove Road.

Village Inn. Beoley.

Cross and Bowling Green. Bransons Cross.

The Brook Inn. Elcocks Brook.

Fleece Hotel. Ballinger, C. Crabbs Cross.

The Royal Oak. Blundell, S. Crabbs Cross.

Yew Tree Inn. Briney P. Haycutter. Feckenham.

The Old Rose and Crown Inn. Dyer, W. H. Feckenham.

Lygon Arms. Sprosen, F. R. Feckenham.

Eight Bells. Beer Retailer. Styler, W.

Green Dragon Inn. Byrne, J. M. Sambourne.

The Griffin Public House. Studley.

Swan Hotel. Feast, W. J. Studley.

Royal Oak Inn. Hopes, W. T. H.

Needlemakers Arms. Huband, J. E. Studley.

Shakespeare Inn. Ireson, W. Redditch Road, Studley.

Railway Inn. Studley.

The Rising Sun. Mr Edginton. Alcester Street, Redditch.

Nags Head. Sealey, H. Alcester Street.

Cricketers Arms. Hanson, J. Beoley Road.

Waggon and Horses. Russel, W. Beoley Road.

Scale and Compass Inn. Carwardine, H. Birchfield Road.

Seven Stars. Davis, E. H. Birchfield Road.

Queen's Head. Webb, B. Bromsgrove Road.

Jubilee Inn. Ness, J. H. Edward Street.

Fox Inn. Spiers Thomas, Edward Street.

Fountain Inn. Mansell, Frank, Richard. Evesham Street.

The Talbot. Snelgar, Reginald. Evesham Street.

Dog and Pheasant Inn. Field, Charles. Evesham Road.

Hungry Man. Mrs Hewitt. Evesham Street. Built 1930.

The Bell Inn. Foster, F. H. Evesham Road. Headless Cross.

The Gate Inn. Hall, Herbert. Evesham Road. Headless Cross.

The White Hart. Hirst, J. H. Evesham Road. Headless Cross.

Railway Tavern. Grove, E. H. Hewell Road.

Jubilee Oak Inn. Futrill, A. E. Ipsley Street.

Alma Tavern. Jeffs, F. W. Ipsley Street.

Warwick Arms Hotel. Shakles, P. F. Ipsley Street.

Royal Hotel. Smith, A. Market Place.

Black Horse Inn. Masters, J. W. Mount Pleasant.

The Nags Head.

The Flag. Unicorn Hill.

Crown Inn. Walker, G. E. Feckenham Road, Astwood Bank.

Arrow Working Men's Club and Institute. Steward: W. Malin. Prospect Road.

Kings Arms. Bradnock, C. Beoley Road.

Plough and Harrow Hotel. Charman, Thomas. Mount Pleasant.

Jubilee Inn. Mr William Crook. Edward Street.

Scourer's Arms. Davies, F. Prospect Hill.

Bristol Inn. Davies, Edwin. Birchfield Road, Headless Cross.

Red Lion Hotel. Dorrington, H. Red Lion Street.

Plumber's Arms. Duffin, A. Walford Street.

Greyhound Inn. Edwards, R. Prospect Hill (Fish Hill).
Cricketers' Arms. Edwards, A. E. Beoley Road.
Dog and Pheasant. Field, C. Evesham Road.
Shakespeare Inn. Godson, E. Walford Street.
Unicorn Hotel. Hyde, T. Unicorn Hill.
Foresters' Arms. Jennings, D.
Lamb and Flag. Jones, R. W. Unicorn Hill.
Fox Inn. Mrs Maries. Edward Street.
Scale and Compass. Martin, R. Birchfield Road.
Crown Hotel. Mills, J. Prospect Hill.
Rising Sun. Millward, J. G. 29, Alcester Street.
Seven Stars. Owen, J. Birchfield Road.
Oddfellows' Arms. Partridge, A. Windsor Street.
White Lion Inn. Pinfield, E. Red Lion Street.
Brewers' Arms. Pinfield-Wells, Mrs. Bates Hill.
Alma Tavern. Pye, Frank. Ipsley Street.
Fleece Hotel. Richardson, W. Evesham Street.
Waggon and Horses. Russell, W. Beoley Road.
The Beehive. Sealey, E. Unicorn Hill.
The Railway Hotel. Shelton, Mrs. Unicorn Hill.
Queen's Head. Shrimpton, Mrs S. Queen Street.
Nag's Head. Smith, F. Alcester Street.
Railway Tavern. Stanley, Mr. Hewell Road.
The Lamp Inn. Theay, T. Walford Street.
Licensed Victualler. Mrs Truscott. 9, Albert Street.
Woodland Cottage Inn. Warner, F. Mount Pleasant.
Queen's Head. Webb, Bernard. Bromsgrove Road.
Sportsmans' Arms. Wilkes, A. Peakman Street.
Warwick Arms. Wilshaw, C. H. Ipsley Street.
Bell Inn. Young, Mrs. Britten Street.
Bear Hotel. Taylor. Charles, Mr. Alcester.
Rifleman Inn. Appleby, E. Park Road.
Golden Salmon. Bartlett, A. Evesham Street.
Bell Inn. Cornwall, G. Evesham Road.
White Hart Hotel. Hirst, J. Evesham Road, Headless Cross.
Gate Inn. Kendal, S. Evesham Road.
Royal Hotel. Ledbury, A. Market Place.
Temperance Hotel. Ludford, Mrs. Evesham Street.
Black Horse. Masters, W. 9, Mount Pleasant.
Park Inn. Palmer, Mr. Evesham Road, Headless Cross.
Royal Hotel. Smith, A. Market Place.
Woodbine Public House, near White Hart Public House.
The Lamp Public House. Feasey, Tommy.
The Plumbers Arms. Manning, Ralph.
Outdoor License. Bunch o' Grapes. Hanson, Mr.
King's Arms. Beoley Road.
Bristol Public House. Headless Cross. (Now The Rocklands).
The Fountain Public House. Evesham Street. (Before the Hungry Man).
The Railway Inn. Branden, Billy.
Wagon and Horses. Cull Alan.
The George Public House. Evesham Street was Near Rainscourt's Faggot Shop.

Doctors and Medical
Buckley, Dr. The Woodlands, Evesham Road.
Carpenter, Mrs. Health Missioner. 272, Mount Pleasant.
Mathews, Edward. Surgeon. Prospect Hill.
Pierce, J. E. Surgeon. "Eversleigh", Worcester Road.
Smith, C. C. Surgeon. Church Green East.
Smith, E. P. Surgeon. Prospect Hill.
Smallwood Hospital. Church Green West. Redditch. Matron: Miss Truslove.
Smallwood's Almshouses. Marsden Road. Matron: Miss Wild.

Nurses
Free Nurse Ivor Road.
Mason, Miss. District Nurse. 124, Birchfield Road.
Nurse's Home: Grove Street.
Westbrook Nurse. Nurse's Home, Grove Street.

Police Law Churches Solicitors
Sergeant Best. Church Road.
Broom. Police Constable. 117, Other Road.
Sergeant Colbourne. Church Road.
Superintendent Davies. Church Road.
Stanley, T. J. Police Officer. 8, Mason Road.
Wagstaff Inspector. Police Station, Church Road.
Secondary Education School; Easemore Road.
County Court Office. Prospect Hill.
Fire Station. Park Road.
Jarvis, W. H. M. Registrar Marriages for Alcester. 228, Mount Pleasant.
Wassell, Rev. H. E. R. Easemore Road.
Todd, Rev. E. "Ardenholm" Beoley Road.
Seden: Rev. J. "West Field" Mount Pleasant.
Jeffrey, F. Relieving Officer. Registrar, Births, Deaths. "Crome Dale". 48, Oakly Road.
Pritchard, Rev. J. L. "Wearside", Easemore Road.
Newton, Rev. Canon Religions, "Holmwood".
Bryan, Mrs G. Convent of St Louis. "The Poplars".
Compton, Rev. L. W. The Rectory, Headless Cross.
Crosby, Rev. B. Wesley House.
Fowler, Rev. J. Clement. Beoley Road.
Grant, Rev. Cardross, M. A. The Vicarage, Bromsgrove Road.
Michell, Rev. G. L. 26, Beoley Road.

Solicitors
Browning, E. E. Church Road.
Browning, H. C. Prospect Hill.
Johnson, A. Solicitors. Unicorn Hill.
Kerwood, A. and Son. Prospect Hill.
Thomas, G. Solicitors. Central Chambers.
Tunbridge and Company. Solicitors. 2, William Street.
Whitely, F. J. Solicitors. Unicorn Hill.

Factories

Baylis, T. and Company. Needles and Fish Hooks. 63, Beoley Road.
Baylis, W. and Company. Needle Manufacturers. 70, Oakly Road.
Baylis, W. and Company. Coal Merchants. 70, Oakly Road.
Baylis, J. P. Engineer. 3, Park Road.
Baylis, F. F. Architect. 14a, Unicorn Hill.
Baylis, W. O. Swivel Maker. 31, Oakly Road.
Blackford, J. and Sons. Needle Manufacturers Hardeners and Scourers to the Trade. Lion Works. George Street.
Bott and Thornton. Swivel Makers. Their successors were Allcock Ltd.
Brabant Needle Company. Lion Works. George Street.
Buggins, John and Son. Needles. 18, Mount Pleasant.
Burston, W. and Son. Needle Manufacturers. 187, Mount Pleasant.
Clarkson, D. Swivel Makers. 122, Beoley Road.
Court, C. Needle Manufacturers and Hardeners. 11, Bates Hill.
Crescent Manufacturing Company. Mount Pleasant. Man: Mr C. H. Edmonds.
Gladwell, D. Printer. Easemore Road.
Gould, W. W. and Sons. Needle and Fish Hooks. Feckenham Mills. (Successors to George Webb and Sons. Josh, Warrin. Eagle Mills. Established: 1733.)
Gregg, Geo. and Sons. Printers. Park Road.
Gripp Company. Novelty Works. Lodge Road.
Guillaume Ltd. Needle and Fishing Tackle Manufacturers. Varsity Works, Clive Road.
Hampton, B. Needle-case Manufacturers. South Street.
Harper, Thomas and Sons Ltd. Manufacturers Sewing-machine Needles, Knitting Needles, Crochet Hooks, Needle-cases. Phoenix Works.
Harrison Bartleet and Company. Washford Mills.
Harrison, C. Accountant. Central Chambers.
Harrison, Cyril H. Builder. Oswald Street.
Heath's Springs and Notion Company. Birchfield Road.
Hemming Richard and Son. Needle and Fish Hook Manufacturers. Forge Mills, Prospect Hill.
Hemming and Son Ltd. Needle and Fish Hooks. Windsor Mills, Hewell Road.
Hessin, T. and Company. Needle Manufacturers. Ashleigh Works. 23, Bromsgrove Road.
Hitchman, A. French Polisher. 2, Mount Pleasant.
Hopkins, F. Hook Manufacturer. "Brooklyn" Rectory Road.
Ideal Press. Printers. 74, Evesham Street.
Indicator and Company Ltd. Printers. Easemore Road. Man: Skinner, W. F.
Jakeman, W. Forge Mills.
James, Arthur. Needle and Fish Hook Manufacturers. Excelsior Works, Clive Road.
James, E. Needle and Tackle Manufacturers. Evesham Street.
James. Messrs. Express Works. Evesham Street.
James, John and Sons Ltd. Needle and Fish-Hooks. Victoria Works, Britten Street.
Jameson, William. Sanitary Inspector. Council Offices, Evesham Street.
Laight, C. and Company. Needle Manufacturers. Edward Street.
Lance, P. Machine Pointer. British Needle Mills.
Laugher, W. and Sons. Pin Manufacturers. 118, Beoley Road.
Lewis, H. and Sons. Needle Manufacturers. Victoria Street.
Llewellyn, W. J. Wellington Foundry, Wellington Street.

Long. A. Tinplate Works. Unicorn Hill.
Ludgate Ryder Thomas and Company. Fishing-Tackle. Clive Road.
Ludgate Shaw and Company Ltd. Thimble Manufacturers. British Mills.
Martin Pulverman and Company. Grange Road.
McDonald Teeth and Company. 48, Unicorn Hill.
Melen, W. Swivel Maker. 224, Mount Pleasant.
Metropolitan Engineering Works. Hewel Road.
Milward, H and Sons Ltd. Hand, Surgeons', Sewing-machine Needles, Needle Cases, Fish-Hooks and Fishing Tackle Manufacturers. Washford Mills, Ipsley Street.
Mitchell, Claude. Trafalgar Works.
Mobbs, W. E. Printer. Littleworth.
Monks, E. D. Junior. File and Rasp Manufacturer. Alcester Street.
Moore, G. Tackle Manufacturer. Red Lion Street.
Morrall, Abel Ltd. Needle Manufacturer. Edward Street.
Morris, Alfred and Company. Needle and Tackle Manufacturers Park Road.
Murdoch, C. Baitmakers. 148, Birchfield Road.
Murdoch, T. Bait Manufacturers. Mount Pleasant.
Peel, Harry and Son. Bait Manufacturers. Oakly Road.
Poole, Mrs. Artificial Fly-Maker. 5, Grove Street.
Purcell, John. Harpoon Maker. Oswald Street.
Reading, Turner and Company. Needle Manufacturing. Victoria Street.
Redditch Manufacturing Company. Gresham Works. Redditch.
Redditch Supply Company. 139, Ipsley Street.

Tradespeople

Johnson, A. Butcher. Unicorn Hill.
Johnson, J. J. Upper Grinstey Farm, Headless Cross.
Johnson, J. 2, St George's Road.
Johnson, Mark. Florist. Church Road.

Jones, G. W. Butcher. 17, Alcester Street.
Jones, G. 15, Grove Street. Secretary: Trades Union.
Jones Bros: Drapers. Evesham Street.
Jones, Miss. Milliner. Prospect Hill.
Jones, Harold Ltd. Coal Merchants. Unicorn Hill.
Joscelyne, H. P. Dental Surgeon. "Derrington House" Prospect Hill.
Keyte, Amos. Shopkeeper. 39, Britten Street.
Keyte, F. Umbrella Maker. 60, Evesham Street.
King, Mrs. Bordesley Park Farm.
King, Edmund. Bordesley Lodge Farm. Birmingham Road.
Kings, George. 84, Evesham Road.
Kings, Isaac. Coal Dealer. 37, Lodge Road.
Kings, Mrs I. Dressmaker. 37, Lodge Road.
Kite, E. Boot Repairer. Beoley Road.
Knight, Harold. Smallwood's Arch. Church Green East.
Knight, E. Boot Repairer. 29, Oswald Street.
Laight, Mrs C. Dressmaker. 20, Oakly Road.
Laight, C. and Company. Prospect Hill.
Lankshear, M. Sweet Stores. Church Green East.
Ledbury, J. Cabinet Maker. Wellington Street.
Ledbury, W. Decorater. 104, Evesham Street.
Ledbury, Mrs. China Stores. 104, Evesham Street.
Lee, C. Chipped Potatoes. 139, Ipsley Street.
Lee, F. Bait Manufacturers. Clive Road.
Lewis, A. D. Institute. Church Road.
Lewis, W. Insurance Agent. 197, Evesham Road.
Lewis, Mrs. Dressmaker. 16, Worcester Road.
Lewis, Alfred. Hairdresser. 48, Alcester Street.
Lewis, Henry. J. Drysalter. 37, Alcester Street.
Ludgate. Dairyman. 77, Oakly Road.
Mann, Mr W. Station Master. Unicorn Hill.
Mansfield, H. Bootmaker. 4, Chapel Street, Headless Cross.
Maries, Mrs. Baker. 56, Prospect Hill.
Martin, W. Bootmaker. 49, George Street.
Martin, W. 92, Evesham Road.
Maunton, W. House Furnisher. 99, Evesham Street.
Maunton, F. Sweet Stores. 2, Other Road.
Mayne, R. N. Manager. Electricity Department.
McGilchrist. Newsagent. Alcester Street.
McGilchrist. Milliner. Alcester Street.
McQuay, S. C. Milliner. 14 and 14, Market Place.
Melen, Walter. Fruiterer. 20, Evesham Street.
Merriman, A. Painter. 39, Edward Street.
Metropolitan Bank (of England and Wales) Church Green West. Manager: Mr H. A. Pearson.
Miller, R. J. Capital and Counties Bank, Redditch.
Millward, S. Poulterer, etc. 73, Evesham Street.
Millard, J. A. Painters. Alcester Street.
Mole, D. H. Bootmaker. 92, Evesham Street.
Moore, C. Builder. 15, Mason Road.
Morgan. "Osborne House". Queen Street.
Morris, John. Grocer. 22, Evesham Street.

Morris, Miss K. Dressmaker. 49, Oakly Road.
Morris, F. H. Draper. 217, Mount Pleasant.
Morris, S. Grocer. 18, Ipsley Street.
Mott, Edward G. Grocer. 45, Prospect Road.
Moule. W. Ltd. Chemists. 28, Evesham Street.
Mousley, J. Chemist and Druggist. Alcester Street.
Munslow, Miss. Wine and Spirit Merchant. Post Office. 46, Evesham Street.
National Telephone Company. Church Green East.
Neasom, Mrs. Birchensdale Farm, Salters' Lane.
Neasom and White. Auctioneers. Church Road.
Nelson, J. and Sons Ltd. Butchers. 9, Evesham Street.
Newbold, F. Builder. Easemore Road.
Newman, W. Baker. Marsden Road.
Niblette, W. J. Bootmaker. 42, Prospect Hill.
Noakes, A. Wardrobe Dealer, Pawnbroker. George Street.
Noakes, E. Grocer. 45, George Street.
O'Neal, Mrs W. H. Dressmaker. Mount Pleasant.
Orme, Miss. Newsagent. 82, Evesham Street.
Owen, J. Insurance Agent. 124, Beoley Road.
Palmer, J. Bootmaker. 139, Other Road.
Palmer, C. Baker. 19, Alcester Street.
Palmer, Cecil. Watchmaker and Optician. 10, Evesham Street.
Parry Mell Motor Company. Easemore Road.
Parsons, Eli. Pianoforte Teacher. 53, Bromsgrove Road.
Partridge, S. and M. E. Dressmakers. 3, St George's Road.
Payne, E. Baker. 177, St George's Road.
Pears and Company. Ladies' and Childrens' Outfitters.
Pearkes Stores. 41, Evesham Street.
Peart, Mrs E. M. 4, Church Green.
Peasgood, Thomas. Old Farm. Beoley Road.
Perkins, L. Chipped Potato Salesman. Unicorn Hill.
Perrins. Architect. Evesham Street.
Perry, J. W. Grocer. 48, Beoley Road.
Perry, F. Draper. 102, Evesham Road.
Picture Palace Ltd. Alcester Street.
Pipers Penny Bazaar. Evesham Street.
Pitt, H. General Smith. 6, Red Lion Street.
Pitts, A. L. Cycle Stores and Motor Garage. Evesham Street.
Ralph, G. F. and Son. Furniture Removers. 23, Alcester Street.
Rea, Mrs W. Milliner. 71, Lodge Road.
Read, F. Horse-breaker. 147, Evesham Street.
Read, W. Horse-breaker. Royal Hotel Mews. Market Place.
Roberts, Mrs. General Dealer. 97, Ipsley Street.
Robinson, W. Grocer. 141, Evesham Road.
Roland, George. Dairyman. 8, Melen Street.
Rollins, A. E. Builder. 62, Birchfield Road.
Rose, F. W. Blacksmith. Ipsley Street.
Sage, J. R. General Draper. 2, Bates Hill.
School of Art. (Government) Church Road.

Scorza and Olivieri. (Wine Merchants) 31, Evesham Street. Manager: Mr A. H. Chatterley.

Scott, J. and Company. Drapers. Market Place.

Scriven, Mrs M. A. Stationer. 45, Evesham Street.

Sealey, L. Photographer. 16, Other Road.

Sealey, L. Lamp Dealer. 107, Ipsley Street.

Sealey, P. W. Watchmaker. 56, Evesham Street.

Sergeant, W. Butcher. 139, Evesham Road.

Shakespeare, E. General Dealer. George Street.

Shakles. F. Dairyman. Bridley Moor Farm.

Shrimpton, T. Fancy Draper. Alcester Street.

Silk and Company. Coal merchants. Unicorn Hill.

Sillery, W. Ironmonger. Evesham Street. (Successors to W. Gibbs and Son.)

Simmons, William and Son. Insurance Agents. 14, Unicorn Hill.

Simon, G. Hairdresser. 100a, Evesham Road.

Sisman, Miss. Dressmaker. Factory House. Queen Street.

Skinner, Mrs. Pawnbroker. George Street.

Smith and Spencer. Mineral Water Manufacturers. Ipsley Street.

Smith, Albert. Shorthand Teacher. Easemore Road.

Smith, Mrs. Hairdresser. 27, Alcester Street.

Smith. Baker. 65, Evesham Road.

Smith, Henry. Grinsty Farm. Webheath.

Smith, Mrs. General Dealer. 14, Peakman Street.

Smith, T. 102b, Evesham Street.

Smith, W. Bootmaker. Evesham Road.

Smith, J. W. Insurance Agent. 30, Mason Road.

Smith, T. Fruiterer. Evesham Street.

Smith, T. Bootmaker. Church Green East.

Smith, Mrs. Linemaker. 3, Wellington Street.

Smith, W. H. Motor Cycle Garage. 42, Evesham Street.

Sollis, J. Butcher. George Street.

Spencer, Miss H. Dressmaker. Ipsley Street.

Spencer, G. Watchmaker and Jeweller. 16, Evesham Street.

Spencer, Mrs. Piano Warehouse. 53, Evesham Street.

Squires, R. Electrician. 105, Other Road.

Stanley, Mrs. Provision Dealer. 24, Edward Street.

Stanley, A. J. Grocers. Hewell Road.

Star Tea Company. Market Place.

Terry, W. Photographer. 91, Evesham Street.

Tillesley, G. Grocer. 99, Marsden Road.

Thomas, Misses. Fancy Drapers. 17, Evesham Street.

Thompson, B. R. Butcher. 51, Alcester Street.

Thornton, R. D. Draper. Evesham Street.

Thornton, John. Chemist. Evesham Street.

Tillsley, J. Coal Merchants. 107, Other Road.

Tomlinson, W. J. Electrician. 160, Mount Pleasant and Central Chambers.

Tongue, Edgar. Coach Builder and Wheelwright. Clive Road.

Tongue. Bootmaker. 28, Britten Street.

Tongue and Maddocks. Drapers. 93, Evesham Street.

Turner, Miss. Insurance Agent. 14, Mount Pleasant.

Viles, F. H. Grocer. 129, Evesham Road.

Vincent, D. Dental Surgeon. Church Green West.

Wall, W. Ironmonger, etc. 107, Evesham Road.

Walmsley, F. Clothier. Unicorn Hill.

Ward, T. Grocer. 70, Birchfield Road.

Ward, J. Boot Dealer and Coal Merchant.

Watkins, E. L. Confectioner. 13, Evesham Street.

Watson, J. Watchmaker. 87, Evesham Street.

Watton, Reuben. Gate Works. Hewell Road.

Webb, R. W. Cycle Depot. Church Road.

Webb and Company. Confectioners. The Parade.

Webb, T. E. and Sons. Bakers and Corn Merchants. Church Green East.

Welsbourne, J. Butcher. 13, Market Place.

Wells, Mrs. Wine Merchants. 95, Evesham Street.

West, G. Insurance Agent. 6, Oakly Road.

Whites Restaurant. Unicorn Hill.

White, Walter. Marine Stores. Alcester Street.

Whittington, W. Lodging House. Red Lion Street.

Whiteman, J. Hairdresser. Unicorn Hill.

Whitmore, Mrs. Cavendish House, Evesham Street.

Whittle, J. E. Bootmaker. 12, Market Place.

Wilkes, R. Shoemaker. 66, Birchfield Road.

Wilkes, H. Newsagent, etc. Park Road.

Wilkes, Mrs. General Dealer. Mount Pleasant.

Wilkinson. Piano Agent. 36, Alcester Street.

Willetts Bros. Butchers, Evesham Street.

Williams. A. Confectioner. 86, Evesham Street.

Williams, F. General Dealer. 60, Edward Street.

Williams, F. Watchmaker and Jeweller. 54, Alcester Street.

Willmore, N. Broker. Unicorn Hill.

Wright and Company. 97, Evesham Street.

Wright, W. J. "Inglewood". Birchfield Road.

Wright, J. Carpenter. 155, Evesham Road.

Wyers, C. and Sons. Painters. Prospect Hill.

Yorke, F. W. Architect. Ivor Road.

Young, F. Butcher. 63, Evesham Street.

Young, W. Carpenter. Birchfield Road.

Young, E. Butcher. 139, Evesham Road.

Lewis. Faggots and Peas. Beoley Road.

Bonaker's Puddings. Red Lion Street.

Bon Bon, Evesham Street.

Bint, Mrs. Wool Shop. Evesham Street.

Bourne, Miss. Dressmaker. 51, Birchfield Road.

Baylis, T. W. Dairyman. 93, St George's Road.

Baylis, Mrs E. Dressmaker. Alcester Street.

Boyd, Mrs. Mudie's Library. Church Green West.

Bradley, Misses. Confectioners. Prospect Hill.

Bradley, Miss. Dressmaker. Prospect Hill.

Clayton, A. Central Stores. Mount Pleasant.

Horen, P. Union Club, Easemore Road.

Industrial Co-op and Company. 95, Evesham Street.

Indicator Company Ltd. Printers. Easemore Road. Manager: Mr W. F. Skinner.
Indicator Company. Stationery Department. Prospect Hill.
Ireson, W. A. Newsagent. 127, Evesham Road.
Ireson, F. Stationer and Post Office. 127, Evesham Road.
Jakeman, W. Workmans' Club. Prospect Road.
Kuck, N. Needle Pointer. 10, Queen Street.
Ladbury, R. B. Fruiterer. Alcester Street.
Ladbury, E. and Company. Motor Garage, 40, Alcester Street.
Laugher, W. H. Engineer. Smith Street.
Lawrence, A. H. Boot Factor. Alcester Street.
Lea, Benjamin. Grocer. 38, Evesham Road.
Liberal Club. Alcester Street.
Lilley, H. Poultry Farm, Holloway Lane.
Lilley, H. Hairdresser. 23, Unicorn Hill.
Lindhal, L. Plumber. 192, Mount Pleasant.
Liptons Ltd. 17a, Evesham Street.
Pretty, Mrs. Baker. l, Birchfield Road.
Priddey, Miss. Stationer, 15, Beoley Road.
Murdoch, J. S. Tailor. 143, Evesham Road.
Mustin, A. E. Draper. Evesham Street.
Mutton, D. J. Tailor. 143, Evesham Road.
Myers, A. Fruiterers, etc. Alcester Street.
Myers and Son. Florists. 139, Evesham Street.

Some of the old places that have now become extinct

Avon Terrace, Birmingham Road.
Pound Yard.
Clarke's Yard, Alcester Street. (Near Select Cinema).
The Parade.
Chapel Street, Headless Cross.
Rectory Road, Headless Cross.
Archer Road (Redditch College of Further Education).
Mason Road, Headless Cross.
Monk's Building, Ipsley Street.
Highfield Road, Headless Cross.
Harris's Lane.
Grange Road.
Beoley Mill Cottages, Beoley Road.
Smallwood Row, off Peakman Street.
Phillips Terrace off Beoley Road.
West Street.
Old Birmingham Road.
Parsons Row.
Adelaide Street.
Silver Street. (Charlie Field's abode). Hill Street.
Hill Street, Littleworth.
Bates Hill.
Clive Avenue, Birmingham Road.
Kathleen Place, Evesham Street.
Catherine's Place, Evesham Street.
Izod's yard, Evesham Street.

Red Lion Yard, Red Lion Street.
Hill's Yard.
Pool Place, Near Ipsley Street.
Hemming's Entry, Prospect Hill.
Fish Hill, (Crown Inn).
Hill's Yard off Unicorn Hill.
Hill Street off Prospect Hill. Elm Road, Near Bridge Street.
Batson, R. 5, Clarke's Yard.
Croxall, Thomas. 24, William Street.
Cull, J. L. Union Street.
Cuttriss, T. J. 2, Avon Terrace, Old Birmingham Road.
Danks, E. 18, Hill Street, off Unicorn Hill.
Davies, Miss. 8, Almshouses, Marsden Road.
Davy, W. Wellington Street.
Daw, W. Monk's Buildings, Ipsley Street.
Day, David, L. Walford Street.
Day, Mrs. 1, Unicorn Hill.
Day, George. Holloway Lane.
Deaner, A. 3, West Avenue, South Street.
Devey, Mrs. 7, Phillip's Terrace, Beoley Road.
Deville, Miss. 22, Unicorn Hill.
Dobbins, Richard. 5, Adelaide Street.
Dolphin, H. Mayfields Mount Pleasant.
Dolphin, John. 28, Albert Street.
Dosher, James. 156, Mount Pleasant.
Doyley, Christopher. 32, Prospect Road.
Ducrow, Mrs. George Street.
Duggins, E. 1, Britten Street.
Durden, George. Brockhill Lane.
Dyer, Mrs. Silver Street.
Evans, T. Harrington House, Park Road.
Smith, T. Wapping.
Faithful, Alfred. 111, Mount Pleasant.
Faulkner, T. 62, Marsden Road.
Faulkner, T. 78, St George's Road.
Faulkner, Mr. 91, Marsden Road.
Ford, Mrs. Hill's Yard. Prospect Hill.
Fourt, H. 16, Charles Street.
Fowler, Felix. 20, Windsor Street.
Francis, A. back 7, Britten Street.
Whadcoat, F. Jersey Cottages. Prospect Road.
Wheeler, A. E. Holmdene. William Street.
Wheeler, Henry. Clark's Yard.
Whitehouse, James. 2b, St George's Road.
Whittington, W. Lodging Road, Red Lion Street.
Whitmore, Mrs. Cavendish House, Evesham Street.
Wilkes, G. Mayfields, Mount Pleasant.
Williams, Alfred. The Birches. Headless Cross.
Willis, John. The Mount, Hewell Road.
Woodfield, Mrs. Elmsdale, Hewell Road.
Woodfield, W. and Sons. Needle and Fishing Tackle "Easemore Works" Bridge Street.
Wooley, H. Palm Maker. Clive Avenue.
Wormington, Philip. Salters Lane.
Worcestershire Model Laundry. 41, Unicorn Hill.
Worth, G. Arran House, Church Green.
Wright, G. and Sons. Fly Dressers. Forge Mills.

Wright, John Frederick. 50, Prospect Hill.
Yates, Mrs Senior. back 39, Evesham Street.
White's Restaurant. Unicorn Hill.
Buckley, Mr. Gorton's Arch, off Church Green East.
Cemetry Road was off Plymouth Road.
Hill Street off Unicorn Hill. Near Granny Ross's Pawn Shop.
Golf Links. Soudan, off Plymouth Road.
Guise, Mrs. back 3, Market Place.
Haden, Mrs. back 45, Unicorn Hill.
Field, Mrs. Smallwood's Arch, Church Green.
Glossop, S. 4, Margaret Place, Queen Street.
Gold, Mrs. (Veterinary Service) Smallwood Row.
Goldby, Mrs S. 10, St Phillip's Terrace, Beoley Road.
Ross, Annie (granny) 29, Unicorn Hill (1929 Almanack).
Union Street was off Lodge Road (Alkaline Batteries).
Easemore Lane was a continuation of Easemore Road. Now Abbey Dale Estate.
Ross Mary Lizzie. Clarke's Yard.

Places in Redditch at that Time

Cedar Road. Elm Road. Bridley Moor Road, off Hewell Road. Sillins Avenue. Farm Road. Arthur Street. Stevenson Place, off Beoley Road. South Street. Batchley Road. Oak Tree Avenue. Hazel Road. Willow Way. Hawthorne Road. Foxlydiate Crescent.
Beecham, F. 6, Grove Square, Walford Street.
Beck, G. back 44, George Street.
Bint, W. back 36, Evesham Street.
Blackford, G. back 113, Evesham Street.
Calcombe, Mr. "Inglewood". Birchfield Road.
Wright (Timber Merchants) Margaret. "Inglewood" Birchfield Road.
Canning, Mrs. West Avenue.
Candy, F. 4, Beaufort Street.
Carr, J. Harris's Lane.
Chambers Alfred. back 69, Evesham Street.
Chellingsworth, F. Brockhill Lane.
Clark, James. back 21, Ipsley Street.
Coates, E. J. Beoley Mill Cottages.
Coleman, J. Almshouses. Marsden Road.
Cooper, A. H. 5, Smallwood Row, Peakman Street.
Court, Mrs S. A. 3, Margaret Place, Queen Street.
Court, W. Vaynor House, Evesham Road.
Cox, William. 6, George Street.
Cox, Fred. 12, Izod's Yard.
Cox, Samuel. Silver Street.
Cox, S. The Cottage, Littleworth.
Craddock, Mary Mrs. 1. Mount Pleasant.
Craddock, John. Ipsley Street.
Craddock, Howard. 3, Pound Yard.
Crook, John. 1. court. 3, Evesham Street.
Crook, Mrs. 1, Clark's Yard.

Crow, Edwin. Archer Road.
Crow, George Garibaldi. Beaufort Street.
Crow, S. Clive Avenue, Old Birmingham Road.
Gardener, W. 3, Arrow Road.
Gazey, Mrs. 253, Beoley Road.
Gibbs, Mrs. Silver Street.
Gibbs, Henry. Red Lion Street.
Glossop, S. 4, Margaret Place, Queen Street.
Goddard, Benjamin. 25, Adelaide Street.
Goodlet, Alexander. 24, Park Road.
Goswell, T. 8, Peakman Street.
Gregory, Silas. 30, William Street.
Grier, Mrs. 10, Unicorn Hill.
Griffiths, W. 25, back Victoria Street.
Grose, Mrs. Boston House, Worcester Road.
Grose, Miss. Grafton House School, Worcester Road.
Guise, Mrs. back 3, Market Place.
Gurden, Eli, Beoley Road.
Haden, Frank. back 45, Unicorn Hill.
Harber, R. Kathleen Place, Evesham Street.
Hardman, H. 31, Millsborough Road.
Harris. "Aberdom", Easemore Road.
Harris, Ephraim. 27, Mount Pleasant.
Hawkes, W. back Cricketer's Arms, Beoley Road.
Hawkeswood, W. 25, Skinner's Buildings, George Street.
Hearn, Mrs. 9, Izod's Yard.
Heath, E. A. Hemming's Entry, Prospect Hill (Fish Hill).
Hemming, Mrs. 'Le Chalet', Feckenham Road.
Hemming, Mrs. 3, Kathleen Place, Evesham Street.
Herberts, Miss E. George Street.
Hill, Eli. Herbert Square, George Street.
Hill, George. Clarke's Yard, Alcester Street.
Hobday, T. 'Arron House', Church Green East.
Holliday, John. Muscatt's Way.
Hollington, John. Bridge Street.
Holmes, Walter. 2, Ipsley Row.
Houghton, G. Salter's Lane.
Houghton, W. "Anglemount" Worcester Road.

Redditch Names of That Period

Lady Eleanor (hairdresser) Amy, Isabella, Sarah Ann, Eliza.
Gentlemen: Abel, Caleb, Edgar, Hiriam, Joseph, Isaac, Edmund, Joshua, Eli, Samuel, Claude, Benjamin, Felix, Edwin, Harold, Amos, Daniel, Rupert, Ephraim.
Edwin drove the Co-op horse with the baker's delivery.
Huins, S. L. "Lyncombe", Park Road.
Hunt, J. 45, Walford Street.
Hunt, A. 91, Robinson's Square, Evesham Road.
Hustwayte, F. Prospect Road.
Jacques, C. 10, Izod's Yard.

Jenkins, Charles. 55, Red Lion Square.
Jennings, G. Viola House, Park Road.
Jills, E. back 17, Alcester Street.
Johnson, Mrs. 'The Rookery', Birchfield Road.
Jones, Harold. Hawthorne Cottage, Birchfield Road.
Kaye, H. 'Evelyn Cottage', Birchfield Road.
Kettle, H. Holloway Lane.
Knight, Joseph. Silver Street.
Ladbury, Miss S. A. 40, Albert Street.
Laugher, W. H. Engineer, Smith Street.
Layton, Mrs. 3, Church Green East.
Layton, J. 2, Bridge Street.
Locke, Charles. Old Toll Gate, Birmingham Road.
Mallam, W. Junior. 151, Evesham Street.
Maries, A. 9, Skinner Street.
Marshall, T. (Town Crier) 3, Victoria Street.
Martin, H. 11, Mason Road, Headless Cross.
Mason, Miss. (District Nurse) 124, Birchfield Road.
Merry, William. back 26, Edward Street.
Messenger, G. 8, Red Lion Street.
Mills, James. Hill Street.
Millward, S. G. back 51, Unicorn Hill.
Millward, G. 13, Skinner Street.
Mitchell, T. 21, Glover Street.
Mogg, John. 2, Skinner's Buildings, George Street.
Moore, Miss. Littleworth House.
Moore, H. 16, St Luke's Terrace.
Moran, Mrs. 5, Izod's Yard, Evesham Street.
Morgan, Harry. 40, Grove Street.
Newall, Mr. 1, Charles Street.
O'Neal, Mrs Susan. 8, Clive Road.
Oscroft, T. 12, Market Place.
Palmer, J. 82, Evesham Street.
Parker, Mrs. 7, Worcester Road.
Parker, Walter. "Stowe", Clive Avenue, Birmingham Road.
Parsons, M. Clifton House, Ipsley Street.
Payne, Charles. 14, Wellington Street.
Pearson, H. A. Church Green West.
Peart, Mrs E. M. 4, Church Green West.
Penrice, E. Bentley Gables, Rectory Road.
Perks, B. "The Rye", Easemore Road.
Petford, T. 2, Kathleen Place, Evesham Street.
Portsman, W. 99b, Evesham Street.
Prescott, William Fergus. 15, Windsor Street.
Purcell, T. 3, Adelaide Street.
Purcell, Henry. 14, Warwick Place, Ipsley Street.
Roach, A. S. 68, Unicorn Hill.
Roberts, Mrs. (General Dealer) 97, Ipsley Street.
Ross, E. Clark's Yard.
Rose, George. The Cottage. Worcester Road.
Rowley, Benjamin. 6, Pound Yard.
Russell, A. Leah Place, 87, Prospect Road.
Rust, J. 155, St George's Road.
Seden, B. The Hut, West Avenue.
Sillery, W. The Barn, Birmingham Road.
Skinner, Mrs. "Hazelwood", Holloway Lane.

Slater, C. Littleworth House.
Smart, Mrs. Gorton Arch, Smallwood's Row, Peakham Street.
Smith, John. Webheath Lane (later Heathfield Road), Webheath.
Snape, J. Portland Place. 93, Prospect Road.
Stanley, W. Weight's Farm Cottage.
Strain, Arthur (Junior). Beoley Cottages.
Stratford, William. 1, Queen Street.
Stratton, J. Old Mill House, Windsor Road.
Street, John. Hill Street.
Styler, Arthur. Marlpit Lane, Headless Cross.
Styler. back 21, Walford Street.
Sutton, Mrs Minnie. 145, Ipsley Street.
Swan, F. 11, Silver Street.
Talbot, William. Pound Yard.
Taylor, H. 2, Grove's Square. Walford Street.
Taylor, Mrs. 12, Hill Street.
Taylor, William. Church Green East.
Terry, George. 1, Izod's Yard.
Thomas, Terry. 8, Izod's Yard.
Thick, William. 55, Oakley Road.
Tongue, F. 93, Robinson's Yard.
Tracey, J. 25, Victoria Street.
Tranter, B. Factory House. Prospect Hill.
Urry, W. 56, Glover Street.
Twimbro, J. 24, Red Lion Street.
Uglow, H. R. 44, Marsden Road.
Vale, Sydney. back 1, Alcester Street.
Vale, A. 22, Church Green East.
Vaughan, W. 3, Grove's Buildings, Walford Street.
Walthew, A. Salop Road.
Walton, Alfred. 8, Silver Street.
Waring, B. Junior. 5, Kathleen Place, Evesham Street.
Welsh, Mrs. back 7, Britten Street.
Whadcoat, F. Jersey Cottages. Prospect Road.
Wheeler, Henry, Clarke's Yard, Alcester Street.
Williams, Alfred. The Birches, Headless Cross.
Willis, John. "The Mount", Hewell Road.
Worth, G. "Arran House", Church Green East.
Yarnall, Mrs Dorcas. 5, Unicorn Hill.
Yates, Mrs B. back 4, Church Green West.
Yoxall, Mrs M. C. Orchard Street.
Taylor, Albert. 123, Walkwood Road, Hunt End.
Taylor, W. H. Hemming's Entry. Prospect Hill (near Crown Public House)
Lewis, Mr. 17, Greenlands (Previously Beoley Road)
Emmes, Nancy. Beoley Road.
Widows, Nancy. Beoley Road.
Chisholm, Mrs. Beoley Road.

Names of Local Girls
Amelia, Dorcas, Jesse, Lavinia, Emma, Polly.

Names of Local Boys
Gabriel, Herbert, Emanuel, Isaiah, Victor, Augustus, Cecil, Mathew, Mattias, Reuben. Fergus, Timothy, Elijah, Elias, Solomon.

About this time there was advertised in the local paper:

House to let, Birchfield Road, 4 beds, both hot and cold water. W. C. Two reception. Kitchen, scullery. The wording sounded like rooms of a mansion for £30 per annum.

Adelaide Street, to let 3s 6d. per week.

Two modern houses to sell £550 presently at £36. 8s. per annum. Vine Street. Good cottage to let at 3s per week.

It was reported in the local paper of that week that a Mr Albert Wilcox was sued for non-payment to wife and 4 children of 10/-s. per week.

He is reported to have told the magistrate that he couldn't possibly afford this out of his wage of 18/-s. per week.

In the same edition was advertised by the Bromsgrove Union: Female Cook required. Wage: £18 per annum. Full Board, washing and lodging, but no beer.

Gloves were offered at 1¼d per pair. Bedsteads at 9s 11d.

Wicker chairs at 2s 11d. Dining chairs 1s each.

Wringing and mangling machines 20s and 50s.

In the medicine lines there were: Bairds Bilious and Liver Pills from Boots Chemist 3, Evesham Street. Powell's Balsam of Aniseed cures colds. Priced at 1/1½d bottle. Dr. J. Collis Browne's chlorodyne. It purifies and strengthens every organ of the body. St Jacobs oil.

Rheu : Neu : Sci : Stiffness and sprains. 1½d. Guaranteed to conquer pain. Vogelers' curative compound. Holloways' pills and ointments. We were advised to take Laxative Quinine Tablets and all druggists were obliged to give full refund if it failed to cure. Only 1/1½d per tin. Dr Kings Dandelion and Quinine Tablets. Monsoon Bitters and Ointment. Young lady ill for years now cured by this remedy and was now able to walk 8 or 9 miles a day.

Lamps were available from John Dyer. Alcester Street from 4½d up to £5.

For painless extraction of teeth under nitrous oxide gas and other scientific methods consult Mr Whitehead, surgeon, Church Green East. Reduced prices to the working classes and others of limited means.

Redditch Saw Mills. Red Lion Street.

Redditch Electro Plating Company Ltd. Worcester Road. Director: Mr J. Guise.

Rice, Charles. Fruiterer. Unicorn Hill.

Roberts and Lee. Needle and Fish Hook Manufacturers. Prospect Hill.

Rollins and Parker. Golf Works. Feckenham Road.

Russell, T. Cabinet Maker, Melen Street.

Russell Brothers. Littleworth.

Salisbury and Thomas Ltd. Needle Manufacturers. Universal Works, Clive Road.

Sandilands, J. and Sons. Tackle Manufacturers. Bromsgrove Road.

Sarsons, Misses. Bakers. 28, Unicorn Hill.

Sealey, E. Fish Hook Manufacturers. Hewell Road.

Sealey, W. Needlecase Manufacturers. 13, Bates Hill.

Shepard, J. Monumental Works. Ipsley Street.

Shrimpton, J. Builder. 140, Mount Pleasant.

Shrimpton, E. A. Coal Merchant. 19. Worcester Road.

Shrimpton, Alfred and Sons. Needle, Fish Hooks, Fishing Tackle Manufacturers. Britannia Works, William Street.

Shrimpton, T. and Sons. Needle Manufacturers. 50, Edward Street.

Shrimpton, Z. and Sons. Needle and Crochet Hook Manufacturers. Britannia Works, William Street.

Shrimpton, Emanuel and Fletcher. Surgeons' Needle Manufacturer. Queen Street.

Simpson. Vulcan Works, Park Road.

Singer Manufacturer Company. 51, Evesham Street.

Smith Brothers. Beoley Mills.

Smith, Albert and Company. Dominion Works, Ludlow Road.

Smith, W. and Sons. Manufacturers, Sailors and Sailmakers' Palms. Needles, Tools and Leather goods. Neptune Works, Beoley Road.

S. P. A. R. Manufacturing Company Ltd. Toledo Works, Peakman Street.

Spencer, Charles. Netting, Tambour Sail Needle Manufacturers. 50, Edward Street.

Standard Needle Company. 11, Worcester Road.

Stanley, M. Upper Grinsty Farm.

Steele, T. Baker and Butcher. 31, Alcester Street.

Stokes, Frederick. Old Farm, Beoley Road.

Street, H. Sweets and Cafe. Market Place.